Principles and elements of

MEDIEVAL CHURCH ARCHITECTURE

in Western Europe

Michel Henry-Claude, Laurence Stefanon and Yannick Zaballos
With the collaboration of Sylvie Fournier, agrégée de Lettres
Illustrations : Laurence Stefanon and Antoine Rego
Translation : Beryl Degans

- les éditions **Fragile** -

MILESTONES

	HISTORICAL EVENT		ARTS & ARCHITECTURE
300			
	PALAEO-CHRISTIAN		
313	Edict of Milan, freedom of worship accorded to Christians	**c. 326**	Constantine has a basilica built over the Sai Peter's tomb in the Vatican
Beg. Vth cent.	The great invasions	**529**	Rule of Saint Benedict of Nursia
476	Fall of the Roman Empire in the West	**End VIth cent.**	*Historia francorum*, Gregory of Tours
Before 500	Clovis converted to Christianity	**VIth-VIIth cent.**	Founding of numerous churches and monas teries in Gaul
	CAROLINGIAN PERIOD		
c. 715	Maximum of Muslim territorial expansion in Spain	**VIIth-VIIIth cent.**	Irish illuminated manuscripts (Lindisfarn *Gospels* and the *Book of Kells*)
726	Start of the iconoclastical quarrel in Byzantium	**755**	Council of Vez organizes the community of ca nons around the bishop, reorganization of th interior of cathedrals (chancel)
768-814	Reign of Charlemagne		
800			
843	Treaty of Verdun, partition of Carolingian Empire	**816-817**	Monastic Reform by Benedict of Aniane
IXth cent.	Norsemen raid France	**c. 821**	Einhard, *Vita Caroli*
910	Guillaume of Aquitaine founds Cluny Abbey	**c. 830**	Plan of the future monastery of Saint Gall
911	Treaty of Saint Clair-sur-Epte, foundation of the Duchy of Normandy		
929	Spain : creation of the Caliphate of Cordoba	**957**	Church of Banyoles (Catalonia) vaulted in stone
	ROMANESQUE PERIOD		
987	Advent of the Capetians in France	**End Xth cent.**	First example of ambulatory* with radiating chapels, Clermont Ferrand
989	"Peace of God" decreed by the bishops of Aquitaine (Council of Charroux)	**End Xth cent.**	Use of diagonal* ribs in Armenian churches
End Xth cent.	Height of the Byzantine Empire Beginning of feudal system in France		
1000			
1016	Council of Verdun-sur-le-Doubs urges the lords to respect the "peace of God"	**1020**	Reappearance of human figures in monumenta sculpture (lintel of St. Genis des Fontaines)
c. 1020	Council of Orleans "peace of God" revived	**1062-1083**	Construction of the abbey church of the Trinity in Caen
1066	Battle of Hastings. William of Normandy conquers England	**1063**	Start of the construction of Saint Mark's on the model of domed Byzantine churches
1073-1085	Pope Gregory VII the Reformer	**XIth cent.**	Building in stone becomes general
1085	Capture of Toledo by the Christians	**1075-1080**	Appearance of historiated capitals at Sain Sernin church in Toulouse
1096-1099	First Crusade		
1098	Founding of the Cistercian Order by Robert de Molesmes	**1093-1128**	First use of diagonal* ribs at Durham
1100			
Early XIIth cent.	First borough charters	**c. 1100**	Building of the cloister* gallery at Moissac (firs historiated cloister)
1119	Founding of the Order of Templars	**c. 1120**	Sculpted tympanum of Moissac
1119	Council of Toulouse condemns Catharist heresy	**c. 1120-1130**	Sculpted tympanum of Conques
1122	Concordat of Worms. Emperor Henri V renounces investing bishops which remains papal prerogative.	**1120**	Vezelay : use of groin* vaulting over the centra aisle
		1120-1178	Saint Front of Perigueux (line of domes)
		c. 1130-1140	Sculpted tympana of Autun and Vezelay
		c. 1130	Sexpartite vaults at Saint Etienne of Caen
	START OF GOTHIC PERIOD		
1137-1180	Reign of Louis VII	**c. 1141-1144**	Reconstruction of the choir of the abbey church of Saint Denis
1146	Saint Bernard preaches the Second Crusade	**Mid. XIIth cent.**	Royal portal of Chartres
1147	Regency of Suger during the Second Crusade	**c. 1150**	Start of building of Notre Dame of Noyon
1152	Marriage of Henry Plantagenet & Eleanor of Aquitaine	**c. 1155**	First apparent flying buttresses (St. Germain des Prés)
1154	Henry II Plantagenet, king of England	**c. 1160**	Start of the construction of Notre Dame of Laon
1180-1223	Reign of Philip Augustus	**c. 1180**	Romanesque facade of St. Trophimes of Arles
1189-1192	Third Crusade	**c. 1185**	Choir of abbey church of Pontigny
	CLASSICAL GOTHIC PERIOD		
		1195-1220	Construction of the choir of the nave of Notre Dame of Chartres
1200			
1203	Fourth Crusade	**c. 1200**	Start of the building of Notre Dame of Rouen
1204	Conquest of Normandy by Philip Augustus	**1220-1236**	Building of the facade and nave of Notre Dame of Amiens
1209-1229	Crusade against the Albigensians		
	RAYONNANT GOTHIC PERIOD		
1215	Founding of the Dominican Order. Council of Lateran IV which affirms the supremacy of spiritual power over the temporal	**c. 1230**	Villard de Honnecourt's Sketchbook
1248-1250	Seventh Crusade	**1247-1275**	Building of the choir of Saint Pierre of Beauvais
		1257	Founding of the Sorbonne
		1275-1292	Building of the nave of the Jacobins at Toulouse
1270	Death of Saint Louis during the Eighth Crusade	**1284**	Collapse of the choir of Beauvais
1300			
1309	Clement V first Pope in Avignon	**1309-1424**	Building of the Palace of the Doges in Venice
1312	Dissolution of the Order of the Temple	**c. 1312**	Dante, *Inferno*
1328	Valois dynasty reigns in France	**1334**	Start of the construction of the campanile of Florence by Giotto
1337	Start of the Hundred Years' war		
1346	Battle of Crecy	**1334-1342**	Building of the first Palace of the Popes at Avignon
1348	Black Death ravages Europe	**1350-1353**	Boccace, *Decameron*
	FLAMBOYANT GOTHIC PERIOD		
1364	Consecration of Charles V	**1370**	Charles V commissions the Bastille
1378-1417	Great schism of the Western Church	**1375-1381**	Tapestry of the Apocalypse (Angers)
1400			
1415	Battle of Agincourt	**1400**	Jean Froissart, *Chronicles*
		1410-1416	The Limbourg brothers illustrate the Duc of Berry's *Très Riches Heures*
1438	The Pragmatic Sanction of Bourges defines the authority of the King of France over the bishops of the realm.	**1455**	First printing of the Bible by Gutenberg
1453	Siege and capture of Constantinople by the Turks and end of the Hundred Years' War	**c. 1470**	Start of the building of the church of Notre Dame de l'Epine

LATERAN BASILICA (ROME)
Founded by Constantine* (IVth cent.)

SAINT MICHEL-DE-CUXA
Consecrated in 974.
Transformed mid XIth century.
Equipped at first with an atrium* and a second belfry*.

BAPTISTERY OF SAINT JEAN, POITIERS
Built mid. IVth century, restored VIth century and Xth century.
Surmounted on the outside by a pediment.

SAINT-MARTIN-DU-CANIGOU

Consecrated in 1009.
Lombard* bands on the apse, two apsidals and the campanile.

NOTRE-DAME, JUMIÈGES

Consecrated in 1067 in the presence of William the Conqueror, destroyed after 1804. One of the large Romanesque churches (nave 88 m. long, 25 m. high).

SAINTE-FOY, CONQUES

Abbey church built circa 1030-1080. Interior arrangement (ambulatory with radiating chapels typical of pilgrimage churches) apparent on the apse.

SAINT-SERNIN, TOULOUSE
Only the apse was standing when consecrated in 1096. Double side aisles. Almost entirely built in brick.

CLUNY III

South arm of transept, belfry, as well as a few capitals of the ambulatory are all that remain of the largest of the Romanesque churches (187 m. long, two transepts, five radiating chapels, 12.000 sculpted capitals).

SAINTE MARIE, SOUILLAC
Apse of the abbey church vaulted with a line of domes.
Early XIIth century.

SAINT-GERMER-DE-FLY
1140-1150.
Characteristic of the early Gothic, flying buttresses hidden in the roofspace, cross-rib vaulting.

SAINT DENIS
Harmonic* facade built by Suger* pre-1140.
Necropolis of the kings of France.

SAINT ÉTIENNE, BOURGES
Built between circa 1194-1260
Nave with five aisles without transept and sexpartite vaults.

SAINT RÉMI, RHEIMS
Abbey church consecrated in 1090. Choir built 1170-1200.
Includes an elevation on five levels.
Openwork triforium*.

NOTRE DAME, PARIS
Harmonic* facade built between 1200 and 1220.
Towers completed circa 1250.

WELLS (ANGLETERRE)

1220-1239, 1367-1386, for the South Tower, 1407-1424 for the North Tower. English Gothic rapidly acquired its own specificities : built outside the towns, English cathedrals were very long, increasing their surface without attempting to reach the heights French cathedrals attained.

SAINTE CHAPELLE, PARIS
Built for Saint Louis between 1242 and 1248 without flying buttresses but reinforced by a metallic structure.

SAINTE-CÉCILE, ALBI
Built from about 1276 on. Characteristic of southern Gothic : single aisle, no flying buttresses.

INTRODUCTION

"Each transept includes three aisles of unequal width, separated by square piers of four half-columns bearing the great arcades with their double roll of voussoirs, the transverse ribs of the main barrel vault and those which separate the groined vault from the side aisles."

Marcel Aubert, *The Church of Conques*

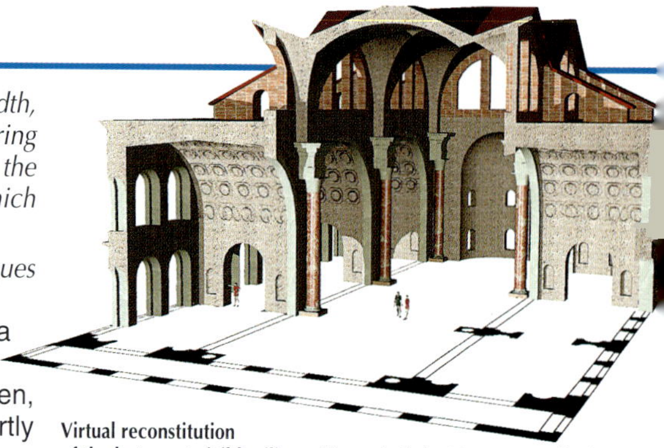

Virtual reconstitution of the last great civil basilica *of Rome built by Maxentius at the beginnin of the IVth century. It is the only Roman basilica vaulted in stone. Its soli vaults give its central aisle a span of more than twenty-five metres, a widt the medieval vaults would never attain. After defeating Maxentius Constantine had a statue of himself nine metres high raised in an apse** ILLUSTRATION PHILIPPE PERROT.

A chancel arch, an ambulatory, a transept, a clerestory, a round arch... All these elements seem more or less familiar to us. But very often, the realities they represent appear elusive; partly because each of these elements designates an object which must be apprehended in three dimensions — but which is often represented only in a two-dimensional form — and partly because behind these objects lies a misunderstood history : that of the monument by which and for which these innovations appeared in medieval religious architecture : the church, or, more precisely, the great church, the basilica*. Because it is present everywhere in the West and seems so familiar, a church is a building we believe we know. But, if it is easy to affirm that a fortress was intended as a place for defence and domination, it is less easy to apprehend the principles that govern the space and plan of a church. What are the necessities its building has to address? Why does a church have a nave, a central aisle, a transept, side aisles? To realize what is really an apse or a choir, to understand what led the master-craftsmen of the Middle Ages to defy the laws of gravity, we must examine the history of this building which is so familiar yet so strange, a history which began early in the IVth century A.D. but which had its roots much further back in time (☛ page 7).

When in 313 A.D., free exercise of their religion was granted to Christians by the Edict of Milan, they were at last able to build their own places of worship. The Christian choice — in which Emperor Constantine* doubtless had a hand — revealed a new conception of divinity and of the relationship of man to divine power. A single emperor, a single god. In order to symbolize in stone the alliance between the new religion and the Empire, the Christians rejected the whole of the architectural tradition of the pagan temples. But they made a strange choice in adopting as a model for their sacred buildings a large secular edifice, which was used in Antiquity as a hall of justice and as a covered market : the basilica*. The fundamental choices were quickly made. Nave, side aisles, apse, transept formed the framework of these new principles and of a new vocabulary (☛ page 8). And despite numerous modifications made to the basilican plan — notably to adapt it to the Christian form of worship (☛ page 10) — from the IVth century A.D. until the end of the Gothic* period — the basilica remained the fundamental model for churches in the western world. This early choice was to determine the history and the originality of western religious architecture. For the basilican plan, unlike the plan with a central dome which was developed in the East from the Vth century, had a basic instability : conceived originally to bear a roof over timberwork the basilica was a **longitudinal edifice** particularly **inadapted to the thrusts*** generated by **cut* stone vaults**.

Until the Xth century, most of the churches in the West had timber frame roofs. But the end of the invasions saw the return of prosperity which, unlike what happened in the Carolingian* period, was to last for a considerable time. This prosperity was accompanied by a sudden increase in population. Many churches had to be built or rebuilt. When the builders decided to equip the new buildings with stone vaults, the particularity of the basilican plan was revealed in all its complexity (☛ insert below). From the XIth to the XIIth century, the paradoxical constraints characteristic of Romanesque* architecture were, on one hand, to achieve a widening of the edifice to accommodate the ever-growing numbers of faithful and pilgrims* and on the other to adapt the nave to stone vaulting, while struggling with great difficulty against the destabilizing forces* generated by the thrust of these vaults (☛ page 14). From the middle of the XIIth century, a revolutionary change took place with the use of a method of roofing hitherto rarely used : cross*-rib vaulting. This would wholly transform methods of construction. The problems generated by thrust* were now largely resolved and in the cities the vaults of Gothic* cathedrals — stiffened on the underside by stone ribs* — rose to heights hitherto unknown and were surmounted by immense glazed openings letting in the light of day (☛ page 18).

** : see index page 36*

FIRE, POWER, AND PLAINSONG...

Although made possible at the end of the invasions by the return of prosperity, the stone vaulting of church naves* which began in the Xth century had various origins and reasons. In addition to its longevity, the main advantage of stone lay in its resistance to fire : unlike former edifices where a flaming timberwork roof on collapsing might bring down the walls, a stone-vaulted basilica did not present the same risk, for the vault was placed between the roof and the interior space. The existence of the vault, offering a permanent "scaffold" could perhaps make easier the maintenance and repair of the timberwork. Added to these technical reasons were those linked to the very role of a church. Infinitely more than a timber frame roof, a vault guides the eye towards the liturgical centre of the basilica. Moreover it can be painted and its form — as well as its name — is a reminder of the heavenly vault (very often the vaults of basilicas were decorated with stars on a deep blue background). One last liturgical argument is found in the importance of plainsong in the Christian religion : it is not only the interior volume of the church but also vaults which give such impressive acoustics to Christian monuments... There exist reasons of a different order : like castle keeps and bell towers, stone vaults were the symbols of the economic power of the ecclesiastical lords (☛ insert page 16) to whom the secular lords made many donations in order to make legitimate their own power. This was the time of the emergence of the feudal system and it cannot be excluded that a certain emulation, even a rivalry, was at the origin of the renovation and sometimes of the complete reconstruction of numerous churches — some of which had been standing for less than fifty years.

1

DEFINITION OF THE PLAN

"A finished edifice shows us at a glance the sum of the intentions, the inventions, the skill and forces that its existence implies."

Paul Valéry, Variété III.

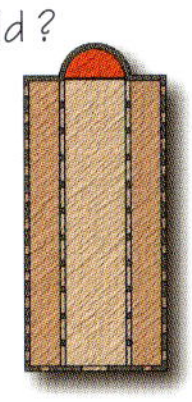

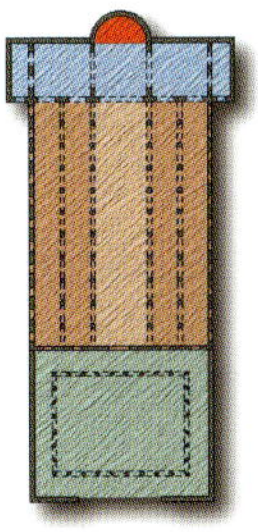

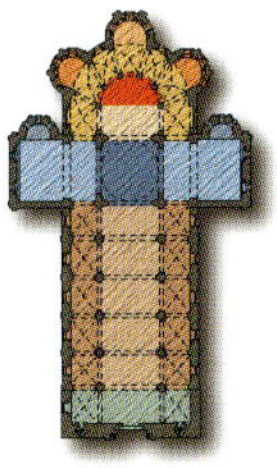

THE PLAN OF A CHURCH (* : ☛ index p. 36)

By convention the plan of a church is represented just above the ledges of the windows and not on floor level. The vaults are shown by unbroken or dotted lines (☛ insert page 27). The designation of the parts of a church is given according to its orientation (☛ page 35). Below : the plan of Saint Etienne Church, Nevers (☛ illust. pp. 16 & 17).

NAVE
- central aisle
- side aisle
- bay of the central aisle
- bay of the side aisle

NAVE. From the Latin *navis*, "a ship", from the Greek *naus*, with the same meaning (cf. *noos*, meaning the central place of a Greek temple). **1.** Interior space of a long building. **2.** In church architecture the word nave used alone designates the longitudinal nave, the part open to the worshippers, situated between the antechurch* and the crossing of the transept (or the architectural choir* if there is no transept). The nave consists of one or several aisles*. Because in smaller churches, a nave has only one aisle, there is often confusion between the words "nave" and "aisle".

AISLE (From Latin *ala* via French *aile*, "wing"). Longitudinal central division of a nave*. The aisle is a long space limited by two walls in the case of a nave with a single aisle, a wall and a colonnade for the side aisles*, and two colonnades* where there is a central aisle. This space is limited in height by a vault and/or a timber roof. The nave and the transept* may be divided into several aisles, a main or **CENTRAL AISLE** (☛ insert page 7) and lateral divisions called side aisles or sometimes collateral aisles (☛ below).

SIDE AISLES (or **COLLATERAL AISLES**, from the Medieval Latin *collateralis*, "at the side of"). Aisles at the side of the nave* or transept* of a church. May also refer to an aisle with a low ceiling, about half the height of the central aisle. This sort of low aisle may be surmounted by a loft or tribune* (☛ illust. below).

BAY. Meaning originally the space included between two supports*. Unity of transversal division of a nave included on the plan between four supports. Bay in elevation : ☛ insert page 14.

LOFT. ☛ page 15. A high gallery (sometimes called a **TRIBUNE**) situated over a low aisle, the whole forming a side aisle* (☛ sketch below).

CHOIR
- apse
- ambulatory
- axial chapel
- radiating chapel

CHOIR (ARCHITECTURAL). From the Latin *chorus*, "choir", as opposed to the LITURGICAL CHOIR* or CHANCEL*. The word choir in a purely architectural sense means that part of the church situated beyond the transept* or beyond the nave* (when there is no transept) and is therefore a simple designation of an architectural part of a church but in its liturgical sense the word carries a different meaning being a place with a specific religious function.

CHEVET (French term for an apse*). From the Latin *caput*, "head". By assimilation of the position of Christ's head on the Cross, this vague term is used to indicate the whole of the walls, windows and roofing of a choir* seen from outside.

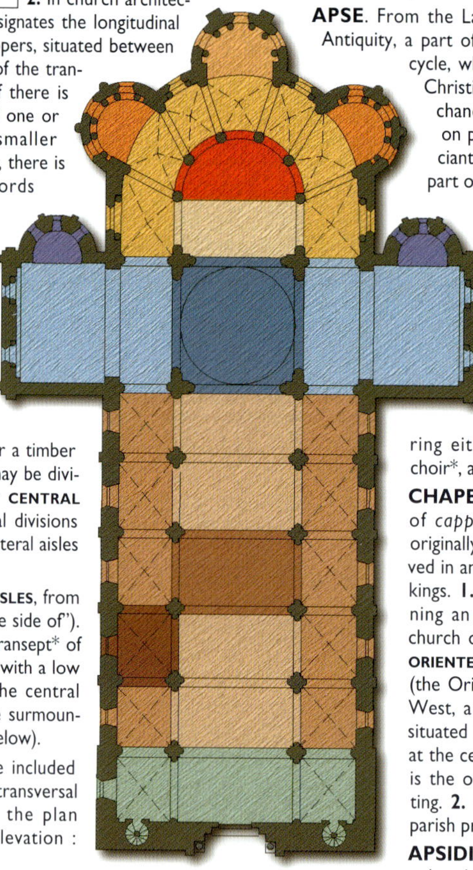

APSE. From the Latin *apsis*, "a wheel, an arch". **1.** In Antiquity, a part of a secular basilica*, forming a hemicycle, where the praetors were seated. **2.** In Christian architecture, the upper part of the chancel of a church forming a semicircle on plan. Appropriated to the highest officiant(s) of the religion, the apse forms a part or the whole of the chancel.

AMBULATORY. From the Latin *ambulare*, to walk about. A winding aisle. Found frequently during the Romanesque period and later in the large churches, the ambulatory allowed the faithful and/or the pilgrims to "ambulate" around the crypt or the chancel* and have access to the radiating chapels without entering either the chancel* or the liturgical choir*, appropriated only to the clerics.

CHAPEL. From the Latin *capella*, diminutive of *cappa*, a "hooded cloak" designating originally Saint Martin's cloak, a relic preserved in an oratory at the court of the Frankish kings. **1.** Room or small aisle always containing an altar* and forming an annex to a church or a secular building. In a church, an **ORIENTED*** **CHAPEL** is a chapel facing the East (the Orient), an **OPPOSED CHAPEL** faces the West, a **RADIATING OR APSIDAL CHAPEL** is situated in the prolongation of a line starting at the centre of the apse*. An **AXIAL CHAPEL** is the only chapel both oriented and radiating. **2.** A small subordinate church without parish priveleges.

APSIDIOLE. A subsidiary chapel* or part of a chapel shaped like a little apse*.

ANTECHURCH

ANTECHURCH. Part of a church on a basilican* plan consisting of the main facade with one or two towers occupying the depth of one or two bays* in front of the nave*. The antechurch often has a porch* or a vestibule within its structure.

PORCH. Hall or gallery communicating with the exterior by openings without woodwork forming a low antechamber in front of the facade. The **PORCH INSIDE THE FABRIC** is a porch integrated into the main antechurch. ☛ NARTHEX*.

TRANSEPT
- arm
- crossing
- oriented chapel

TRANSEPT. Transversal aisle cutting across the axis of some churches between the nave* and the choir* giving them the shape of a cross. The arms* of the transept figure the bars of the Cross where Christ's arms rested. Some churches have several transepts.

CROSSING. The crossing is the space (on plan and **in volume**) defined by the intersection of the central aisle of the transept* with the central aisle of the nave*.

ARM. Each of the parts of the transept on either side of the crossing. They are called north arm and south arm when the church is oriented*.

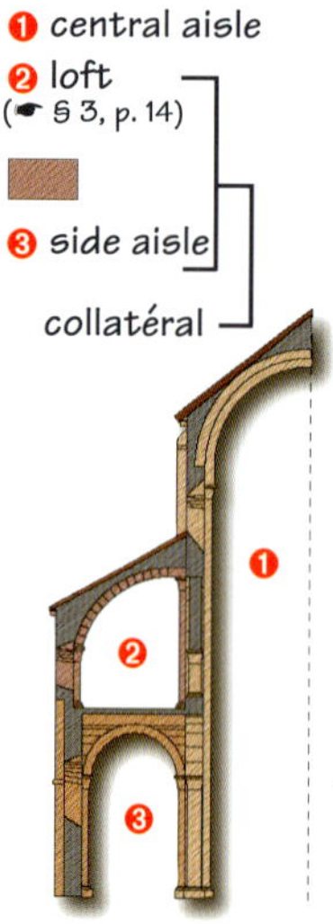

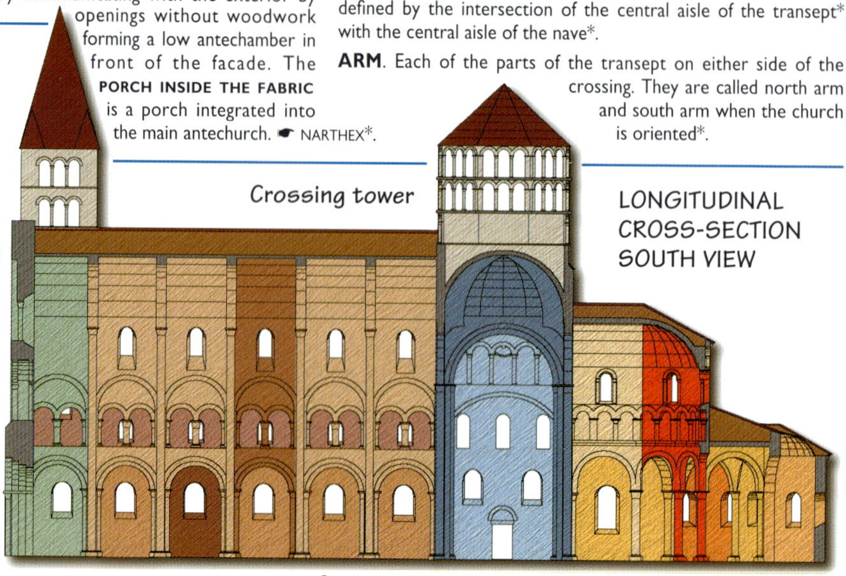

LONGITUDINAL CROSS-SECTION SOUTH VIEW

THE ORIGINS OF THE BASILICAN PLAN

The basilica owes its name to a small edifice built in Athens at the start of the Classical period, the stoa basileios*: the king's portico. The composition of the word itself is indicative of the double origin of the secular Roman basilica.*

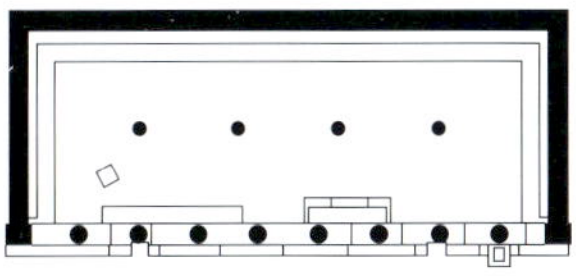

*Plan of the **stoa Basileios** (approx. 15 m. long), to the north-west of the classical agora of Athens (late VIth or early Vth cent. B.C.), where the Athenian laws were preserved — and displayed.*

❶ The basilica is an invention of secular architecture.

In ancient Greece, the agora — public place at the heart of the political and economic life of the cities — was bordered by covered galleries. It was by doubling in depth these galleries that emerged a new type of building at the start of the Classical period : the **portico** (in Greek *stoa*). A double or triple gallery, backing onto a wall or onto a row of halls used either as shops or as chambers (☛ illust. below), the portico was above all used as a passage-way and for receiving a populace whose daily-life was spelled out by what was happening in the agora. Big or small, the porticoes now had multiple functions : covered markets, meeting-places, magistrates' seats, the principle was even applied to the building of storehouses such as the arsenal at Piraeus. In fact, the transforming of galleries (passage-ways) into real buildings underlined the difficult birth of the **very idea** of an **edifice built by the city without being directly dedicated either to games or worship**, but linked to the exercise of civilian life in all its aspects... For example it was under a portico of the Athenian agora, the **stoa *Poikilë*** "the Painted Porch" that Zeno of Citium and his disciples, called **Stoics** — "those of the porch" were to gather...

The very term "**basilica**" comes from *stoa basileios* "the king's porch" (☛ illust. opposite), the seat of the archon-king, a high magistrate of Athens charged with religious responsibilities and with the judging of crimes of impiety and homicide: it was in fact through the amalgam of the general sense of stoa (as a **covered market** used for trading) with the more precise notion of a **seat of high magistracy**, that the civil basilica of Rome would emerge to serve as inspiration to the Christians.

*Virtual reconstitution of the **south Stoa** (agora of Athens). The colonnades opened directly onto the agora whilst rooms were arranged against the back wall.*

❷ The Roman secular basilica sprang from the Greek porticoes but itself introduced two major elements, the apse* and the tie* beam roof.

The first recorded Roman secular basilica is the one built by Cato the Censor circa 180 B.C. A roofed lengthening of the forum and its commercial activities, the secular basilica had a dual function: that of covered market and that of hall of justice. It was a **large rectangular hall**, divided for technical reasons (☛ insert below) into at least **three longitudinal parts** — today called **aisles*** — separated by colonnades which upheld the upper walls of the central aisle*. This latter, higher than the two others with openings letting in daylight was covered by a saddle-roof supported on timberwork with tie* beams, whilst the two side aisles had lean*-to roofs. The ensemble was extended on one or several sides by one or several hemicycles or **apses***. The apse, **the only part of the monument vaulted in stone**, had a specific function: the seat of the praetors during hearings, it was also the seat of authority when the basilica was used as a great assembly hall. Often with a platform leading into it made of wood or even stone — like the one at Pompei — the apse was therefore **closely linked to the notions of authority and justice**.

* : see index page 36

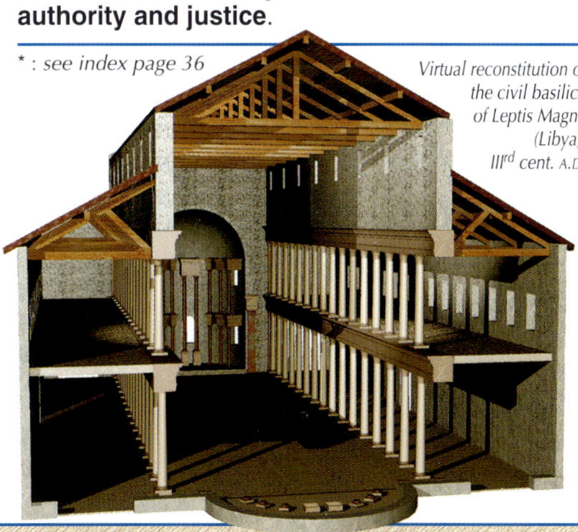

Virtual reconstitution of the civil basilica of Leptis Magna (Libya), IIIrd cent. A.D.

AISLES, SIDE AISLES, MASTERING THE INTERIOR SPACE

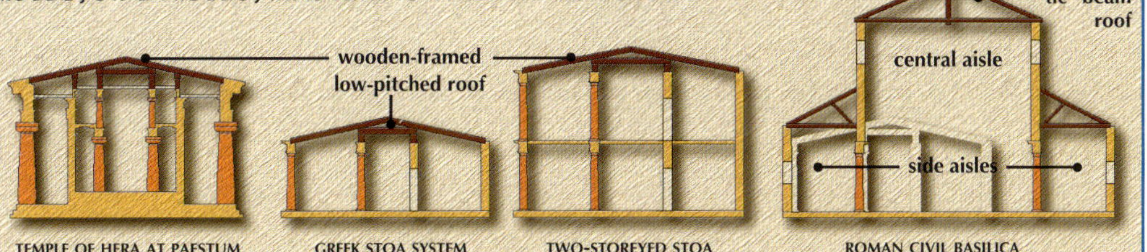

If the timber frame is the simplest means of roofing a longitudinal space, the only method used by the Greeks for their temples and porches was a rudimentary assemblage of props and beams, a technique which did not allow any great width to the space to be roofed (☛ p. 28) without resorting to a multiplication of interior supports (columns or piers). Although used as **assembly-places**, the Greek porches could not defy this rule. It was a Greek or Roman invention which was to allow the removal of the central supports of the timber frame, thus allowing the creation of a volume of larger dimensions. The tie* beam (☛ illust.) made all the parts of the framework interdependent : the central aisle* of a Roman basilica could then attain a width of **more than 20 metres**. In order to widen even more this space, galleries had to be added which explains the existence of **side aisles** (the collateral aisles) in a **basilica*** : in fact, from the origin up to the Gothic* period, the adding of these side aisles was the **only way** to widen the space defined by the **technical limits** of the timber framework or the vault of the central aisle.

THE CHRISTIAN CHOICE

No building of any importance in Christian worship is dated any further back thar the IVth century. However, after 312 the Christian believers were under the protec tion of Emperor Constantine. The choice was then immediate: the Christians re jected the ancient temples and took as model a civil building. The evolution o church architecture in the West was entirely linked to their original choice.*

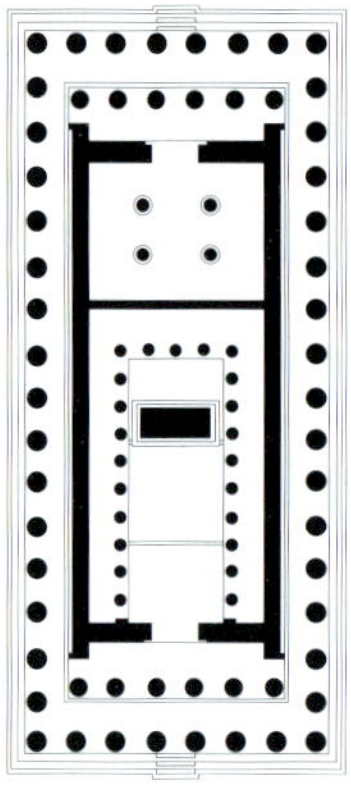

Plan of the Parthenon (dwelling of Athena Parthenos, or the virgin goddess) certainly the most famous of those temples called pagan. The central chamber (the naos) is not more than 10 metres wide. ☛ *insert p. 7.*

❶ *Assembly and power, nave and apse, or the fundamenta reasons for the basilican choice.*

Ekklesia: a popular assembly. The term ecclesia was applied by the Septuagint commentators to the Jewish commonwealth and from them to the Christian Church. The rejection by the Christians of pagan temples in favour of basilicas was brought about by a liturgical upheaval: pagan temples were not built with the intention of housing the faithful during religious ceremonies (☛ illust. opposite), the basilica — a public assembly hall which had acquired a large interior space (☛ insert page 7) — seemed to impose itself upon the Christians now faced with a new obligation to combine the place of **worship** with the place of **assembly**.

But this functional (and liturgical) reason is not the sole explanation for the choice of the basilican plan. For, if the decision to use this great basilican hall sprang from the Christian will to assemble the faithful, the decision to keep the apse*, the seat of the praetors during the exercise of justice — and of authority — was of another intention. The apse became such an integral part of the Christian edifice that it seemed almost inseparable from it. The desire to keep the apse reveals the importance of the original choice: the Christians chose as a model a building linked to magistracy; the house of God was not only a place for prayer but also a tribunal where everyone had to acknowledge imperial law and the authority of the Eternal Judge... and His magistrates (☛ pp. 10 & 11).

Moreover, the basilican choice revealed a new concep tion of the relationship between the divine and the city By its origin (the Greek porches) and by its location (the forum), the basilica had a dual link with the public life o the city. By taking this edifice as a model, the Christians were doing much more than rejecting the temples, they were appropriating a public edifice *par excellence* — which emphasized the very word indicating the Christiar building: in the IVth cent. B.C. the word *ekklesia* designated the assembly of citizens. In the IVth century A.D. it designated the assembly of the faithful o the Christian Church.

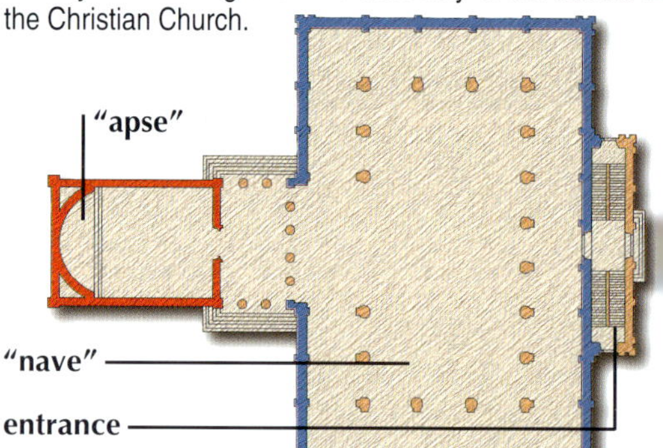

Plan of the secular basilica built by Vitruvius (1st century B.C.) at Fano. Adapted from Claude Perrault Except for the entrance and the apse which were not yet systematically placed on the longitudinal axis of the building, the basilica differs little from the Christian monuments excepting the absence of a transept.*

❷ *The Christians appropriated the basilican plan but adapted it ; their most important transformation was not an addition but a modification of orientation.*

Even before orienting* the basilicas — i.e. in the first meaning of the word, **turning them towards the East** (the Orient from which direction Christ was to come at the end of time) — the Christians modified the arrangement of the **interior volume** of the buildings: until then the entrance of the basilica was situated at the centre of one of the long sides of the building (☛ illust. above) but now the Christians opened the entrance on one of the shortest sides. This change was fundamental: from then on the basilica was no longer just an ordinary edifice, it was a **vessel-like** structure which, from the moment of entry, carried the footsteps, the eyes and the prayers of the congregation towards a single place (☛ illustration below).

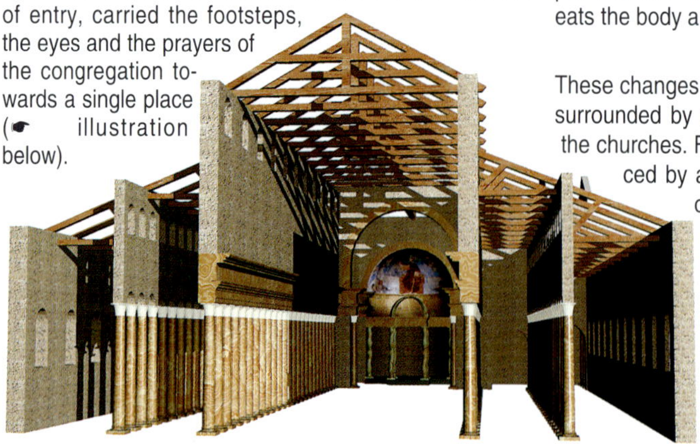

Virtual reconstitution of the elevation of the Basilica of Saint Peter built by Constantine in 326. This building, both imperial and Christian, converges in its entirety towards the magnificence of the apse. The central aisle is 24 m. wide, a width unequalled by the Romanesque* and Gothic buildings to come.*

This place on the other side of the building, where the lines of perspective converge and which was often preceded by a chancel* arch was the **apse*** which became the **very centre of divinity** for the Christians. It was there that Christ in Glory was often depicted. The **seat of the bishop*** would also be installed there. In front of the apse* was the **altar***. Placed in polytheist religions outside the building, the altar now found its place inside the edifice. The sacrifice became symbolic (the lamb was nc longer slaughtered on the altar), but the ritual of mass purification remained (during the eucharist a Christiar eats the body and drinks the blood of Jesus Christ).

These changes brought about others: a square courtyard surrounded by porches, an atrium* appeared in front o the churches. From the Vth century the atrium was replaced by a porch*, the narthex*, beyond which the catechumens (converts who were not yet baptised) could not advance. Another ultimate addition made at the latest in the VIth century was the belfry* whose bells rang out the hours of prayer and summoned the faithful to assemble for devotions. Without doubt, at its origin the belfry was a symbol of domination and an observation post from which the alarm could be sounded in the event of danger.

EAST AND WEST

A fundamental distinction was established as early as the Vth century between the churches of the East and West. In the **Byzantine Empire**, the mastery of domed* vaulting (a technique known for centuries in Mesopotamia and passed on by Persia) led the craftsmen to prefer a centred plan, known as the **Greek cross**, already found in imperial mausolea and thermae. The characteristics of this plan were linked to those of the dome itself (☛ § 2 page 26) and to the implied stability of a centred plan: the central dome is buttressed* by four barrel vaults (these are what give the church the shape of the cross) which easily reduce the thrusts* exerted by the vault and open up a large interior space not made smaller by rows of columns. The Carolingian* and Romanesque* architectures reintroduced into the West the principle of dome construction. But in the Vth century, the absence of such a tradition and the lack of means brought about by the collapse of the Roman Empire privileged the perpetuation of the basilican* plan, easier to build — and less costly — because roofed with timber and not with stone.

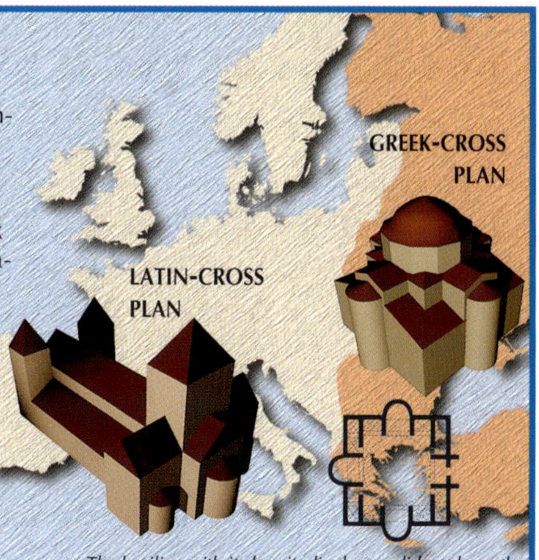

The basilica with its longitudinal nave did not have the stability of the churches built to the Greek-cross plan. It was in fact this major fault which led to its extraordinary transformation during the Romanesque period (☛ pages 14 to 17).

As for the techniques of construction, they remain identical to those of pagan architecture, except that arches* soon systematically replaced architraves* as supports between the upper walls and the columns, a transformation which would progressively lead to the creation of bays* (☛ insert p. 14). But this change was not so much linked to a religious choice as to an evolution of technique initiated several centuries previously, the arch taking a place of increasing importance in architecture (☛ p. 24).

❸ *If the nave was the place of assembly and the apse the symbol of the Christian God, the transept, a fundamental Christian addition, played a more complex part.*

"It is often said that transepts are there to give a church the form of a Latin cross [...] but the laws governing size make their presence essential."

Stephen Jay Gould, *Darwin and the Great Enigmas of Life*, 1979.

The **transept***, which appeared at the origins notably in Saint Peter's at Rome (☛ illustration opposite), emphasized the Christian appropriation of the basilica to which it gave the shape of a cross, the symbol of Christ's Passion. Combined with the chancel* arch in front of it, the transept glorifies the apse* inasmuch as it opens up a space which forces the concentration of perspectives to converge on this precise point of the building. It is a fact that the **interior volume** of an object **increases more rapidly** (cubed) **than its surface** (squared). From this rule of geometry arises the following architectural principle : if the proportions of a small church are multiplied by two, its interior volume is multiplied by four... whilst the surface of the windows allowing in light to this volume is only doubled. It is the **transept** which **makes up for the lack of light**. The transept, the transversal nave*, is closed on its two extremities by gable* walls which do not play a major part in the support of the structure of the church. By passing from a single non-bearing wall (the main facade) to three, the construction of a transept allows for an increased number of doors and windows **without weakening** the structure : it is in the heart of these gable walls that are found the Romanesque wheel* windows and the Gothic* rose* windows (☛ pages 30 & 31). In reality a small church rarely has a transept, unlike the great basilicas. The possibility of making doors in the gable walls of the transept would be fundamental to the coming and going of the faithful through the edifice (☛ pages 10 & 11).

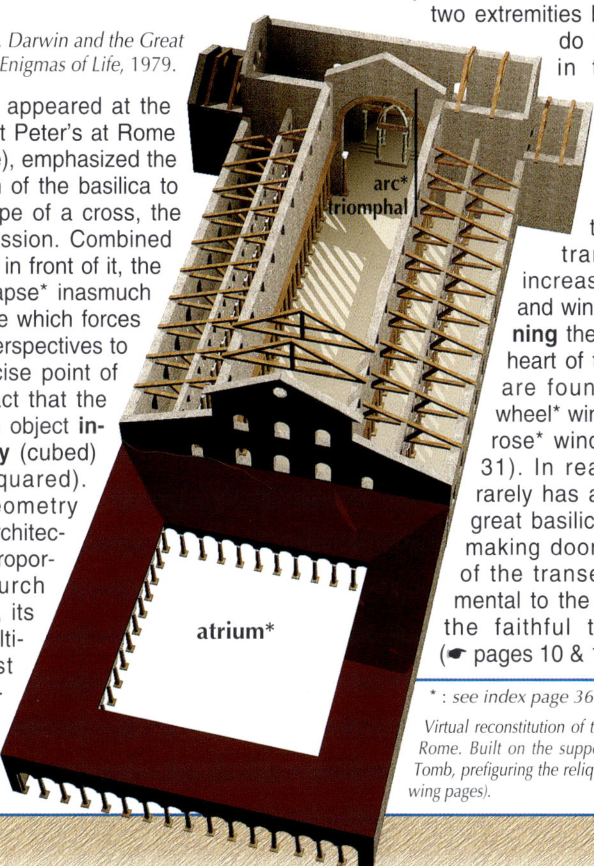

* : *see index page 36*

Virtual reconstitution of the first basilica of Saint Peter at Rome. Built on the supposed site of the Apostle Peter's Tomb, prefiguring the reliquary churches to come (☛ following pages).

MAIN TERMS

ALTAR. From the Latin *altare* meaning a support placed on the table of sacrifices, on the ancient altar (*ara*). In the Christian church, a consecrated table on which the sacrifice of Mass is celebrated. The **HIGH ALTAR**, situated in the sanctuary* is the main altar of a church. Every permanent or moveable altar must have a **SHRINE***, a recess containing relics, sealed off behind a stone.

ATRIUM. From the Latin meaning the main hall of a Roman house, open to the sky at its centre. In Palaeo-Christian architecture, a courtyard surrounded by porticoes* placed in front of a church.

BASILICA. From the Greek (*stoa*) **basileios "royal** porch", the seat of the archon-king at Athens (☛ p. 7). **1.** In ancient times a public building on rectangular plan divided into several parallel aisles, used both as a hall of justice and trading centre. **2.** A church* built on the plan of the Roman basilicas. Within this meaning a cathedral* is a basilica. **3.** In canon law, a church with certain privileges granted by the Pope. Within this meaning, a cathedral is not a basilica.

CHANCEL ARCH. An arch situated at the extremity of the nave, at the entrance of the choir and the transept crossing.

CHURCH. From the Old English *cirice* and the Greek *kyriakon*. **1.** The body of the Christian community. **2.** By metonymy, any place set apart and consecrated for Christian worship (☛ TEMPLE). The evolution of the word may be compared with that of *synagogue*, from the Greek *synagôgê*, "coming together" ; moreover it seems that certain Jewish communities used the basilicas before the Christians adopted the basilican plan.

NARTHEX. **1.** Forepart joined on to the facades of the first basilicas and intended for the catechumens (converts receiving religious instruction but not yet baptised, who were not allowed into the church). **2.** Today the term is often used for the porch on the front of the Romanesque churches.

TEMPLE. Any place of public worship of any divinity.

MAGISTRATES, FAITHFUL & PILGRIMS

Nave, apse and transept formed the general shape of western churches. But the arrangement inside the building was subject to other rules. The church wished to be in the image of the Church, the building in the image of the community: both universal (in Greek katholikos*) and strongly hierarchized.*

❶ *From the origins, it was on the relics of a martyr or a saint that the edifice for Christian worship was founded.*

In ancient traditions the temples belonged to the living and the city. For the dead there was the necropolis (from the Greek *necros, "dead"* and *polis*, "city", "the city of the dead"), situated **outside the towns**, or as in Rome, beyond the holy line, the *pomerium* (*post murum*, "beyond the walls"). The first Christians would be buried in a pagan necropolis (just as tradition holds that Saint Peter was buried on Vatican hill) as well as in the famous catacombs, near the Appian Way.

Saint Peter and Marcellinus, Rome, IVth century. This type of rotunda cemetery church would be set aside in favour of the apsidal basilica (nave, transept, apse) over a crypt.*

At the beginnings of the "official" Christian religion, during the reign of Constantine* when the persecutions were still not far in the past, the Christians created a **new relationship between the place of worship and death**, certainly their first great basilicas were built in the "cities of the dead" but above all on the *supposed sites of the tombs of the saints and martyrs* (from the Greek *martus*, "witness") who, in the image of Christ's suffering on the Cross, were witnesses to God's truth. The cemetery (from the Greek *koimeterion*, "sleeping-place") henceforth became inseparable from the edifice and replaced the necropolis: it was no longer the custom to bury the dead side by side in the cities of the dead but to set them to rest near the venerated saints until the Day of the Last Judgement. At the beginning, the plan used for these "cemetery" churches was a rotunda one (☛ illust. above); the rotunda was in fact a mausoleum (inspired by the imperial mausolea). Soon, however it was the basilican plan without a rotunda which prevailed, but with an **essential addition: the crypt**, under the apse*, which held the remains, the **relics** of the martyr or the saint (his/her bones or, failing that, certain objects relating to his/her life). The Church would not be a mausoleum. But neither would it be only a place of worship to which had been added an assembly place. The **Church was a reliquary*** founded architecturally and spiritually on the presence in its midst of relics and the worship of these was to undergo an extraordinary expansion. The notion that the light of God — which had touched the saint — might touch the faithful through his relics explains in part the importance given to **pilgrimages** in the Romanesque* period and that given to **light** in the Gothic* period.

❷ *The places reserved specifically for the faithful and the pilgrims and the clergy, were organized within the building around the worship of the relics.*

"During the night's vigils, as a great crowd [...] was pressing about the tomb of Saint Martial, more than fifty men and women were trampled down and died inside the church; they were buried the next day."

Adémar de Chabannes, quoted by Georges Duby, *L'An Mil.*

From the beginning of the IVth cent., a suddenly privileged Christianity modelled its structure on that of the imperial administration. In the towns, the church was dominated by **the bishop** (O.E. *biscop*, Latin *episcopus*: "an overseer"). As testifies the term "cathedral", a church where is found the **cathedra** the seat of the bishop. It was the bishop who dominated, preserved and watched over the community, not only in the town but also in a wider jurisdiction, the **diocese** (from the end of the IIIrd century an administrative circonscription of the Empire). The bishop, whose political and civil importance would constantly increase, was sometimes called **hierarch** (deriving from the title of the magistrate entrusted with the imperial cult in the provinces) — a term which through Christianity was to give the word : "hierarchy".

MAIN TERMS

CATHEDRAL. From Latin *cathedra*, from Greek *kathedra*, "bench, seat". A church where the seat of the bishop* is situated and therefore the "mother" of all the churches in the diocese. The greatness of the Gothic* cathedral churches often overshadows the existence of the earlier cathedrals.

CHOIR liturgical. ≠ ARCHITECTURAL CHOIR*. From Latin *chorus*, "chant performed by several singers", from Greek *khoros*, "the chorus of a tragedy". Functional space varying from church to church — and according to the number of clerics. **1.** Space appropriated to the clerics and chorists during Mass. Often railed off and closed on the nave side by the choir-screen. It is furnished with stalls. Possibly raised. **2.** Sometimes the term "liturgical choir" designates the whole of the parts appropriated to the clergy (choir **and** chancel).

CRYPT. From Latin *cripta* and Greek *kriptein*, "to hide". Underground chapel used for burial and containing relics.

JUBE (or ROOD-LOFT). From the first word pronounced by the lector from the platform for benediction before certain lessons : *Jube, Domine, benedicere*. The monumental screen shutting off the liturgical choir* from the nave*, usually surmounted by a loft. First appeared in France in the XIIth cent. (*rood*, old English *rod*, "a cross").

PARCLOSE. **1.** Railing or wall closing off the choir* and the chancel*. **2.** ☛ p. 22. From Latin *per*, "through" and *claudere*, "to close".

RELIQUARY or SHRINE. Precious casket containing one or more relics, from Latin *reliquiae*, "the remains".

SANCTUARY. From Latin *sanctuarium* : "king's cabinet", later "holy place". Part of the church where the high altar is found, appropriated to the highest officiant of the church. In England, also known as the chancel, from Latin *cancelli*, "lattices".

STALL. From Old English *steall*, "a standing-place". Each of the places reserved for clerics grouped in the choir.

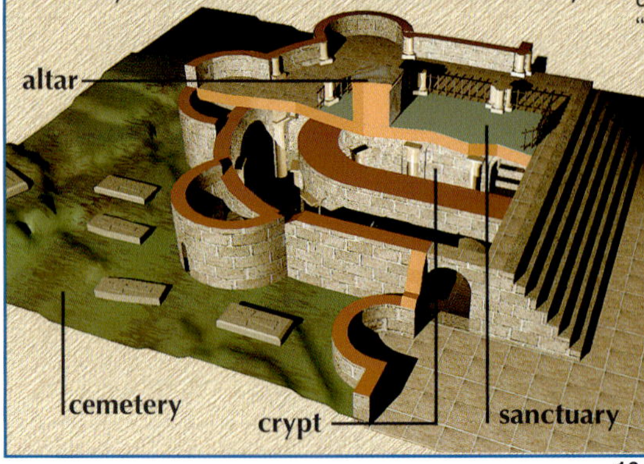

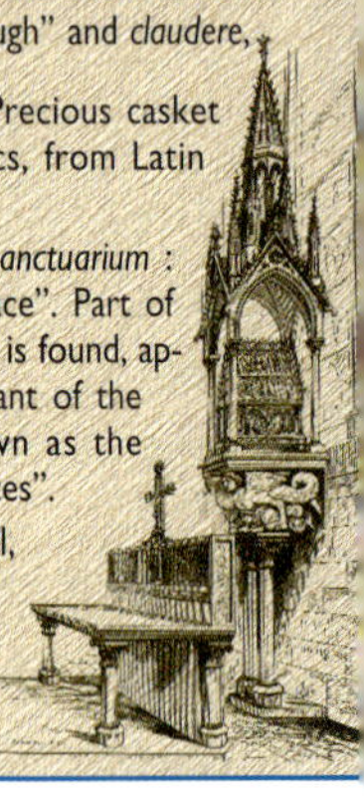

THE CHURCH WITHIN THE CHURCH

The plan of a church is determined by the profound will of a hierarchy which has defined its own position between God, relics and man. To understand the plan of a church, the strict partitioning of the building must be taken into account with the central part (apse and sanctuary, crossing and liturgical choir (or chancel) which alone explains the existence of the ambulatory, the radiating chapels and even the importance accorded to the transept: **the many doors, provided as so many separate ways in and out**. It must, however, be noted that this partitioning which largely disappeared after the Council of Trent*, did not in reality affect the architectural unity of the building. The ancient dream of an *ecclesia*, a community not subjected to a secular authority, was not foreign to this choice.

Example of the interior arrangement in a pilgrimage church

- In **red** sanctuary* or chancel*, and in **blue**, the choir* appropriated to the officiants of the cult.
- In **green** the part where the pilgrims "ambulated".
- In **white**, the nave* appropriated to the faithful.

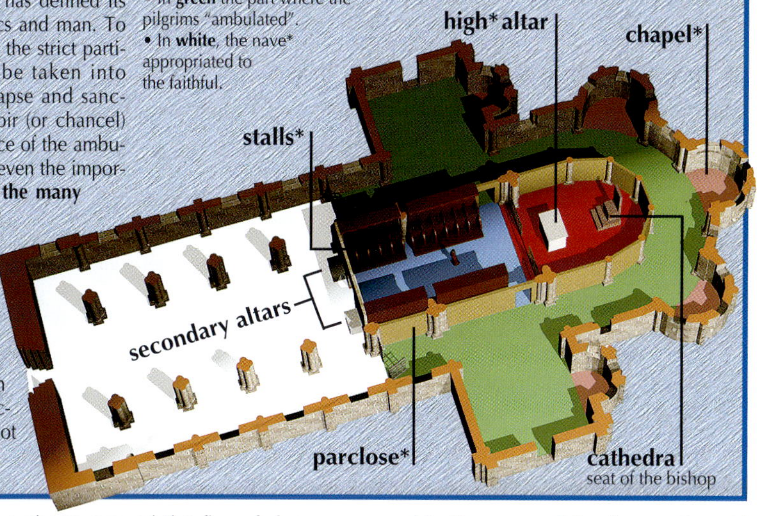

The hierarchy which would take shape around the figure of the bishop was also found inside the building. Originally, semi-circular tiers of seats in the apse were occupied by a council of Elders (the presbyters), who sat round the bishop during ceremonies. This part of the church over the crypt, the **sanctuary*** or chancel*, delimited by a few steps was reserved for the **magistrates of the cult**. In front of the chancel was another reserved place, where the clerics under the authority of the bishop, chanted and prayed during the act of worship: this was the **liturgical choir***. In this way the church was separated into two distinct parts : one the chancel or liturgical choir (the head and the word of the church) reserved for the clergy, and the other the nave* where the faithful were assembled. The separation between these two parts was materialised by the **chancel* screen** (from the Latin *cancellus*, "lattice"). In front of the chancel are found the **ambos** (from Greek *ambôn*, "border") sort of pulpits used for the reading of the scriptures.

This clear-cut opposition (the clergy to the East, the faithful to the West) remained apparent until the IXth century. But the ever-increasing desire of a population, itself constantly increasing, to approach and even **to touch the relics** would shatter this simple arrangement: at the end of the Carolingian period a **new space** was created within the edifice — a space which was to become fundamental in the internal arrangement of the church: the **ambulatory***, a semicircular corridor which skirted round the apse* and itself had small apses, the **apsidal* chapels**. The role of the ambulatory — and of the chapels* — can be seen through the complicated interplay between the clergy, the faithful and the relics : so many chapels, so many secondary altars, so many visible relics. Partly for reasons of security (which had led to the moving of some relics to escape notably from the Norsemen) and partly because of the success of the pilgrimages (which had led to certain religious communities stealing each other's relics), several saints and martyrs were to be found in one church. The ambulatory and the chapels which "radiated" around the apse allowed, on the one hand, a large crowd to reach several saints at the same time, and on the other, allowed the leaders of the cult to preserve a partitioned space, where they could shut themselves off, a **real church within a church**, consisting of the chancel (reserved for the bishop in cathedrals*, or for the abbot* in a monastery) and of the choir (reserved for canons* and monks*). The clergy surrounded this place with a **screen**, a railed or walled enclosure which, from column to column, forbade even the sight of the sanctuary*. In pilgrimage churches, the space was often more partitioned : a railing separated the faithful (who attended the service in the central aisle of the nave*) from the pilgrims (*peregrinus*, "stranger") who by means of doors arranged in the arms of the transept could have access to the radiating* chapels of the ambulatory without coming into contact with the parishioners.

During the Gothic* period, the building of crypts* was abandoned, replaced by a multitude of small added chapels — found even in the nave — in which were displayed richly decorated chests containing relics, called reliquaries. As for the part appropriated to the clergy, it was extended by several bays* towards the back of the church, thus freeing the crossing and the transept. In this way the clergy created an **independent nave** and was even more isolated — the parclose railing could attain five metres in height. A new structure, the **jube*** or **rood-screen**, delimited this reserved space facing the main nave*. Above the jube* stood a cleric, who relayed mass celebrated by the supreme officiant to the congregation of the faithful who could neither see nor hear him. In front of the jube, which replaced the former pulpits, were now placed two altars.

* : *see index page 36*

Sanctuary (in the background, with altar reserved for the bishop), and choir (with canons' stalls*) of Notre Dame of Paris. Viollet-le-Duc,* Dictionnaire raisonné de l'Architecture. *In front of the jube*, (shutting off the choir from the nave*) two altars used by the officiants facing the chancel and not the faithful.*

MAIN PERIODS

"Fine building, by my faith, whose interior and exterior dispositions are reminders o[f] every style. It was at once Byzantine, Romanesque, Gothic [...] with round-arched doors pointed-arched windows, flamboyant rose windows, and fancy spirelets, in a word, ar[n] example of every style [...] it took seven hundred years to build and was successivel[y] shaped according to the architectural fashion of every period."

Jules Verne, *Docteur Ox*

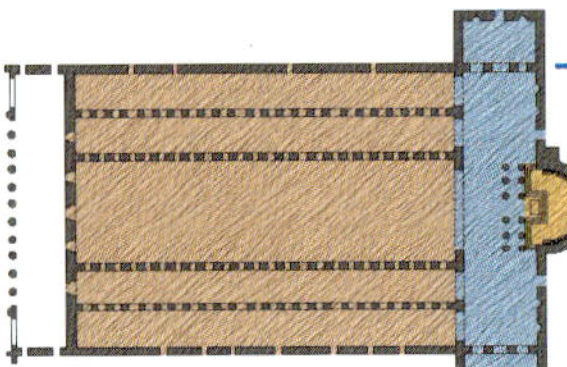

OLD ST. PETER'S IN ROME, EARLY IVth CENTURY.

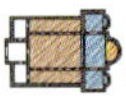

EINHARD'S BASILICA, STEINBACH, c. 820

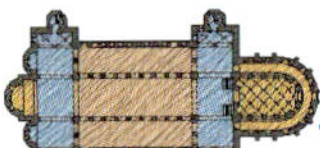

SAINT MICHAEL, HILDESHEIM, EARLY XIth CENTURY.

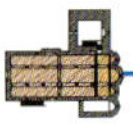

SAINT MARTIN OF CANIGOU CONSECRATED 1009.

Palaeo-Christian Architecture.

After the advent of Constantine*, the decisive choice for a monumental largely imperial architecture was the **basilican plan**: a **huge nave** consisting o[f] five **aisles** separated by **columns, transept, chancel arch and apse**.

Carolingian architecture.

Worship, once dispersed in several buildings (a church to celebrate Mass, a cemetery church, a baptistery and even a double church in the Vth century...) was now united i[n] a **single building** (with a return to an Imperial architecture). A porch — surmounted b[y] chapels* — was often replaced by a second apse. At the end of the period, a decisive disposition was found: **added chapels***, formerly dispersed, were now concentrate[d] around an **ambulatory** or in the **crypt**.

Ottonian architecture.

It did not adopt vaulting in stone; moreover it was notable by the alternate use of pier and columns, and a marked originality in the plan of the buildings: the existence of several transepts and apses, and the west main body called westwork.

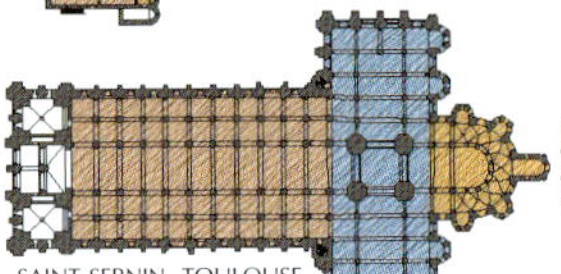

SAINT SERNIN, TOULOUSE c. 1075 - 1120.
BUILT IN BRICK ; THE LARGEST ROMANESQUE CHURCH STILL STANDING.

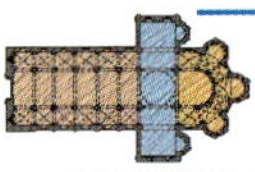

SAINT ETIENNE, NEVERS c. 1068 - c. 1097.

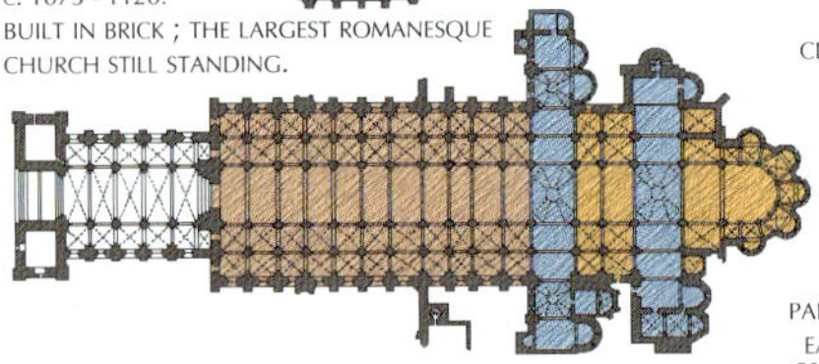

CLUNY (c. 1088 - c. 1120), THE LONGEST ROMANESQUE CHURCH.

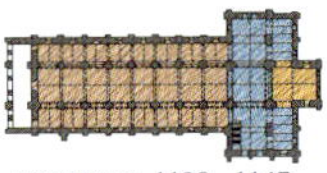

FONTENAY, 1139 - 1147.

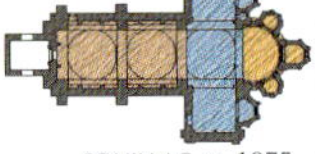

SOUILLAC, c. 1075 - c. 1150.

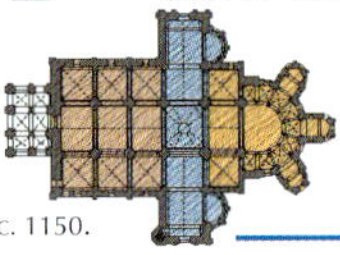

PARAY LE MONIAL. EARLY XIIth CENT.

Romanesque beginnings.

In the second half of the Xth century, there appeared i[n] Northern Italy, then in Catalonia and Burgundy, a revival o[f] building in ashlar*, marked by a **decoration on the outside** – Lombard* bands (pilaster strips) — and by the **first regula[r] attempts at stone vaulting**.

Romanesque architecture. ☛ pp. 14-17

The essential characteristics were the **vaults in cut ston[e]** and the choices made **inside the edifice** to absorb an[d] deviate the thrusts* generated by these vaults. There wer[e] variants according to the region (half-barrel vaults over th[e] lofts in Auvergne and Burgundy, pointed barrel vaults i[n] Provence, absence of vaults in Normandy etc.), but als[o] according to the pilgrimage routes (Saint Sernin an[d] Santiago of Compostela were built in the same style) an[d] sometimes according to the Orders to which they were affiliated (Cluny, Citeaux etc.).

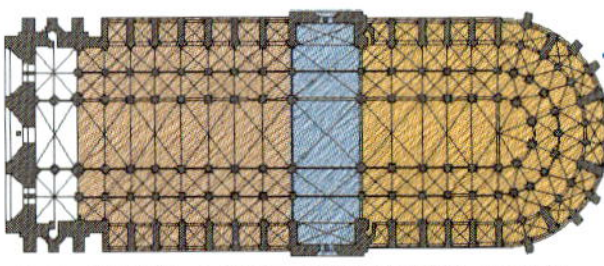

N. D. OF PARIS, c. 1160 - 1220, ALTERED IN 1320.

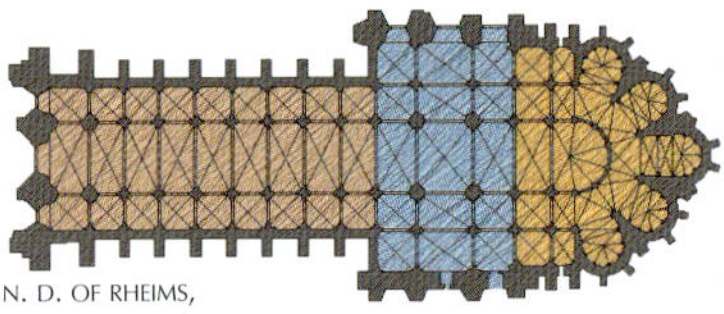

N. D. OF RHEIMS, c.1211 - c. 1260.

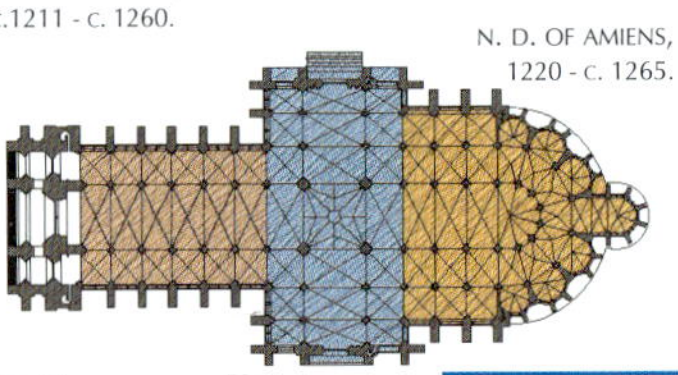

N. D. OF AMIENS, 1220 - c. 1265.

Gothic architecture. ☛ pages 18-21

This used systematically **cross*-rib** and other methods of **ribbed vaulting**, shored up by **flying buttresses**. Walls now had to have openings letting in the **light**.

• **Early Gothic** (1140-1190) corresponds to the elaboration of the founding principles and elements.

• **Classical Gothic** (1190-1230) synthesis of former experiences. Research tends towards an economy of material and towards a greater lighting of the monument

• **Rayonnant Gothic** (1230-1360) gets its name from the rose windows, resembling spoke-wheels, which lighted the churches (*spoke*, "rayon" in French). The triforium* tended to disappear, replaced by huge glazed openings.

• **Flamboyant Gothic** (or **late Gothic**) get[s] its name from the tracery of the window which looked like flames (☛ inser[t] page 31). The tendency towards continuous moulding on piers and arches reduced the importance of capitals.

This chronology represents essentially Norther[n] France. But Gothic art spread to Europe wit[h] certain chronological disparities, and sometimes moving away from the founding principles. Southern France would not adopt Gothi[c] art until the XIIIth century and would giv[e] preference to the hall church style. In Englan[d] **Decorated Gothic** (1250-1350) multiplied ribs and **Perpendicular Gothic** (1350-early XVIth century) whose name derives from the arrangemen[t] of the tracery consisting of perpendicular lines. [It] was singular in its fan vaulting in which the rib[s] figure the bones of an open fan.

0 10 50 m.

The plans are represented on the same scale. The periods are considered exclusively according to their architecture

MAIN TERMS

PALAEO-CHRISTIAN. Relating to the first Christians, from the origins to the VIth century. The term **PALAEO-CHRISTIAN ART** covers two very different realities, that of a **primitive art dating from before the reign of Constantine*** (*art from the catacombs, house of Doura-Europos, the symbols of the good shepherd, of fish, etc.*) and that of **Christian imperial art**, starting with the reign of Constantine*.

CAROLINGIAN. Relating to the Frankish dynasty, which took its name from Charlemagne (Carolus Magnus) and started with the seizure of power by Pippin the Short in 751 ending in 987 with the accession of Hugues Capet.

OTTONIAN. Period and arts relating to the dynasty which ruled in Germany (919-1024) after the extinction of the Carolingian house and which founded the Holy Roman Empire.

ROMANESQUE. From Latin *romanus*, "of Rome". Is used to designate an art (architecture, painting, sculpture, etc.) flourishing in the Latin countries in the late X^th century until and through the XIIth century, even until the early XIIIth century in certain regions (Southern France). Used by the archeologist Charles Duherissier, first in 1818, the term **ROMANESQUE ART** introduced a distinction into medieval art which, until then, was indiscriminately called "Gothic". Comparing artistic development and linguistic evolution, he emphasized the fact that Romanesque art, like the Romance languages, had roots in pagan and later in Christian Rome.

GOTHIC. From low Latin *gothicus*, "relating to the Goths". Adjective first used in a disparaging sense in Italy from the Renaissance onwards. The term was used originally for all medieval art. In the XIXth century, it was used uniquely for the new style which first appeared in Northern France during the decade 1130-1140 and continued until the first half of the XVIth century.

2

MASTERING THE FORCES

"All the processes used throughout the centuries to ensure the stability of buildings can be reduced to two systems: 1° an inert stability, obtained by the simple superposing of materials, as used by the Greeks (...) or like the Romans by binding together concrete masses with mortar; 2° a resilient equilibrium obtained by forces exerting pressure in opposite directions : this system (...) was that of French architecture during the Middle Ages."

Louis Réau, *Dict. d'art et d'archéologie*, art. Stability.

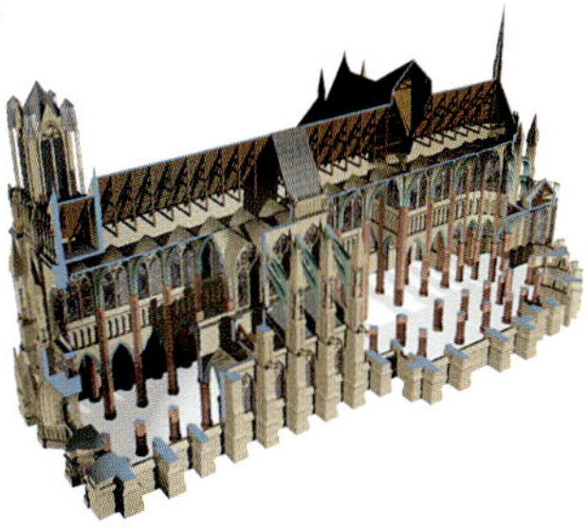

From the end of the Xth century, the nave — a longitudinal space meant at the origi to be roofed by a simple timberwork — was covered with a vault made of adjuste cut stones. The difficulties entailed by this choice were fundamental, for they deter mined the principles of construction of Romanesque* and Gothic* edifices.*

❶ The choice of a vault made of cut stones was crucial; the explanation for its use car be found in the great difficulties of supply of materials and in a shortage of labour.

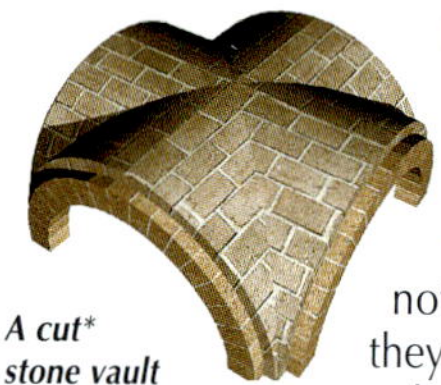

A cut* stone vault *was, like the arch*, an* ***assemblage*** *of wedged* stones or* ***voussoirs****.*

From the Xth century on, for numerous reasons (☛ insert page 4) it became more and more usual to vault churches. But the very first vaults were not always of stone, sometimes they were a mixture of sand, lime and crushed stone closely resembling the **concrete** used by the Romans (☛ illust. pp. 4 & 26). This type of "concrete" vault had an extraordinary advantage: each block "cast" was a **real monolithic unit, exerting no other pressure but its own dead weight***. Nevertheless, the Romanesque builders would reject this process. On one hand, concrete vaults needed a large quantity of raw material — (sand, stone and above all lime — which implied the extensive use of wood, because lime* is obtained by calcining limestone). But on the other hand — and this was probably the decisive argument — the difficulty, even the impossibility, of stocking a larg quantity of raw material entailed recruiting a larg number of men for a relatively short time — whic was possible for an empire, but not for a feudal worlc The much lighter **vault of cut stones** — an assemblag of wedge*-shaped stones which needed only ston available everywhere and a little mortar — and requi red the work of only a few specialists able to cut th stone, the voussoirs* for the vault, **well `efore** it wa set on top of the edifice (☛ pp. 32 & 33). On buildin sites at the beginning of Romanesque art, the wall were often built by local workmen whilst the vaults (a well as the towers) were entrusted to small itinerar teams (such as the "Lombards"). For these specialists i was out of the question to use the concrete vault which demanded a great number of men but little skill The specialisation in crafts, which would soon sepa rate masons from stone-cutters, and the triumph of th "ashlar*" became the fundamental characteristics o medieval architecture (☛ § 2 p. 18).

❷ The lighter cut* stone vaults would one day transform edifices into a lace-work or stone. Nevertheless they held a terrible danger, due to the phenomenon of thrusts*.

Theoretically, a stone vault should transfer all its weight to its supports* (coloured green in the example opposite). But in reality, because the elements (the wedge*-shaped stones or voussoirs*) are independent and their contact surfaces **are necessarily uneven**, this transfer is **not absolutely vertical**; a horizontal force of deviation is generated, level with the supports*, this is called the thrust*. This thrust (in yellow) deviates the whole of the load. The load added to the thrust results in an extremely dangerous **oblique force*** (in red) whose pressure is exerted **all along the length of the vault** and, in the case of a barrel* vault, **along all the length of the nave**. It tends to destabilize the supports* and to push the walls out: should no obstacle or contrary force oppose it, it wil obviously bring about the collapse of the building.

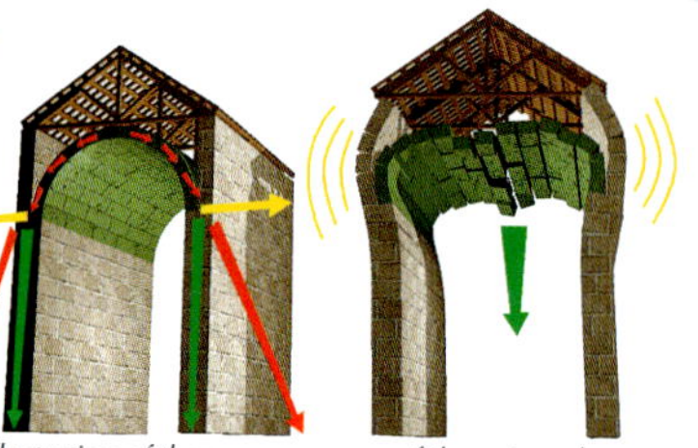

Illustration of the consequences of the outward pressure of the oblique force on the springing of a cut stone vault : without a profound change in the structure, the result is easily foreseen

THE BIRTH OF THE BAY

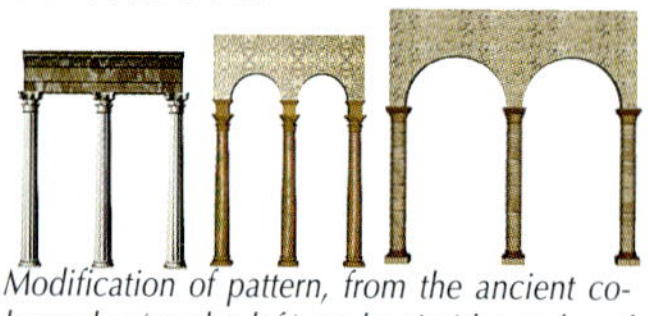

Modification of pattern, from the ancient colonnades (on the left) to the timid arcades of the Constantine period (centre), ending with the great Romanesque arcades* (on the right).*

From the IVth century to the Carolingian* period, the main and perhaps the only technical innovation was that of the evolution of the arch which, breaking away from ancient tradition, took on increasing importance : since it could deviate forces* towards its support, it could increase considerably the span* and so reduce the number of columns needed. Thus was achieved the transition between the rows of columns (ancient colonnades) and the great Romanesque arcades*. This transformation, introducing a new rhythm between bays, arches and supports and the plan of churches, led almost naturally to a new module, which took for its base the span* of the arches* : it was the birth of the bay*. In the Romanesque period, the bay would be the basic unit of the support structure of vaults.

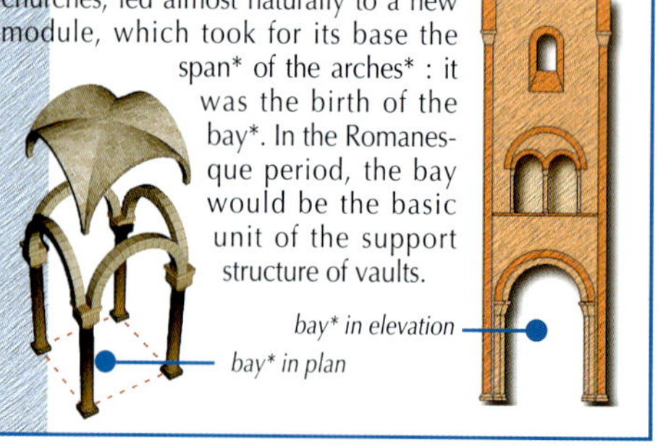

❸ Faced with the phenomenon of thrust*, the Romanesque nave was transformed into a structure of absorption and deviation of forces*.

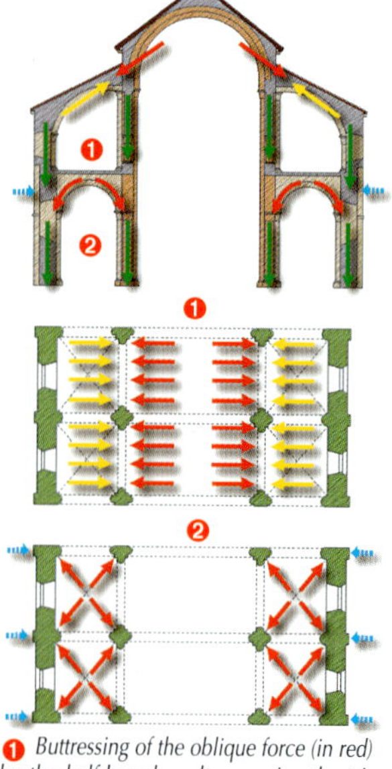

❶ *Buttressing of the oblique force (in red) by the half-barrel vaults covering the tribunes (in yellow)*
❷ *Direction of the pressure of the groin vaults of the side aisles and the shouldering exerted (in blue) by the buttresses*

From bay to bay, a Romanesque nave consists of a series of forces struggling one against the other. To contain these thrusts exerted at the springing of the central vault the system most frequently used (along with a body o other artifices) is the half-barrel vault over **tribunes** or loft (☛ illust. opposite). Whilst the groin vaults of the side aisle strengthen the whole of the construction (n° 2) the half barrels of the tribunes buttress the outward pressure on the central aisle (n° 1). This internal system of deviation o forces is one of the most complete; it has, however, a grea disadvantage inherent to mos Romanesque buildings: **fo fear of seeing the nave collapse, the builders no longer pierced any windows... now the only light coming into the central nave was that from the side aisles***.

❹ The Romanesque processes all tended to reduce oblique* forces to loads* i.e. to reduce a force exerting an outward pressure to a simple dead weight.

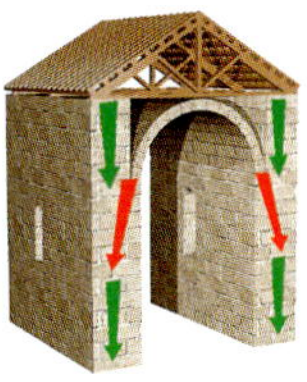

❶ absorption of the outward thrust

The simplest way to counteract the outward thrust exerted on walls was to make them **thicker** : the increase of the load* contains the **oblique* force** generated by the vault (in red) **at the heart of the construction**. This thickening of the wall is accompanied by a **decrease in the size of the openings**. It is one of the constants of Romanesque architecture.

❼ loading on the haunch

This technique shows that the issue is not to lighten the edifice but to reduce the oblique* forces to vertical forces ; to **load the haunches** is to create an added weight which, pressing down onto the springing of the vault, generates an oblique force which, in its turn, deviates the oblique force of the vault and re-balances the whole.

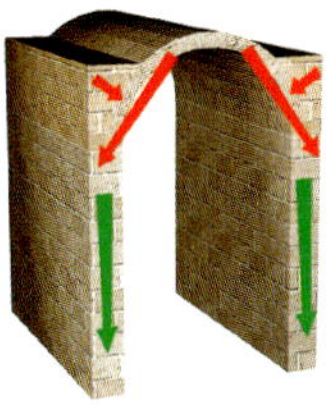

❷ shouldering the edifice

Counterforts* allow — but only from point to point — to counter the outward thrust by their thickness. A counterfort is an instrument of **buttressing*** but not of shouldering*.

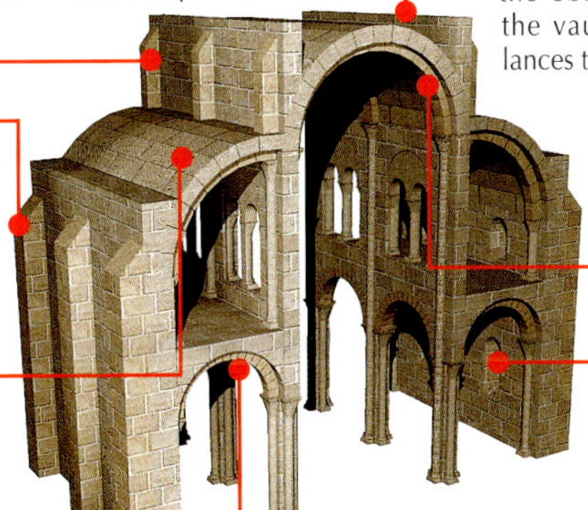

CENTRAL AISLE UNDER SEMICYLINDRICAL BARREL VAULTING

No means is sufficient in itself, it is the integration of several solutions which is characteristic of Romanesque edifices. Neverthless, the major process remains that of half-barrel vaults over tribunes* (n° 3).*

❸ contrebuter

Contrairement à un contrefort, un contrebutement exerce une force active. Ici, le **demi-berceau* de la tribune** s'appuie à la base de la voûte du vaisseau central et engendre **une poussée*** qui dévie la force* oblique. Cette technique est la raison d'être des tribunes* d'une église romane.

❻ supporting

The **transverse* ribs** have a fundamental role : they support the vault in precise points (from bay* to bay) and relieve it from a part of its weight ; they are often coupled on the outside with counterforts*.

❺ increasing the load*

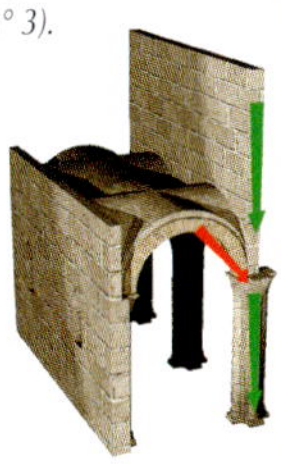

Here the oblique forces of the vault of the side aisles* (in red) are reduced, deviated by the weight of the wall (and the vaults, timber frame and roofing) of the central aisle* (in green) They are thus transformed into simple loads*.

❹ concentrating the forces on precise points

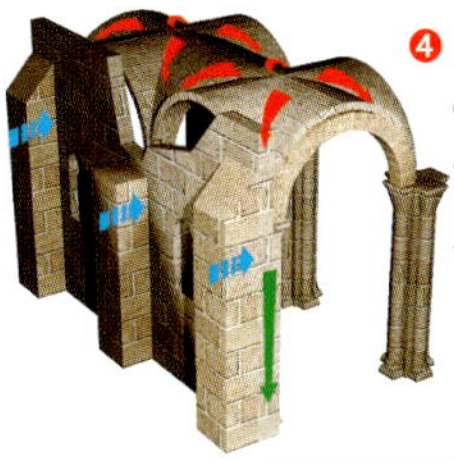

Groin* vaults, frequently used in vaulting side aisles* — but rarely in that of the central aisle — (☛ below n° 1) have the particularity of concentrating the forces on precise points... those where the counterforts are in place, ☛ n° 2. They are also used to strengthen the supports of the central aisle.

ADDED SOLUTIONS

The technique which consists of using half-barrel vaults as buttresses for the central aisle was far from being the only Romanesque solution. Below are a few examples of the cancelling of forces.

❶ central aisle under a groin vault

Because only with difficulty can they span a space of more than eight metres, groin vaults are only belatedly used and rarely used over the central aisle. The appearance of ribs* would resolve this difficulty.

❷ central aisle under transversal barrel vaulting

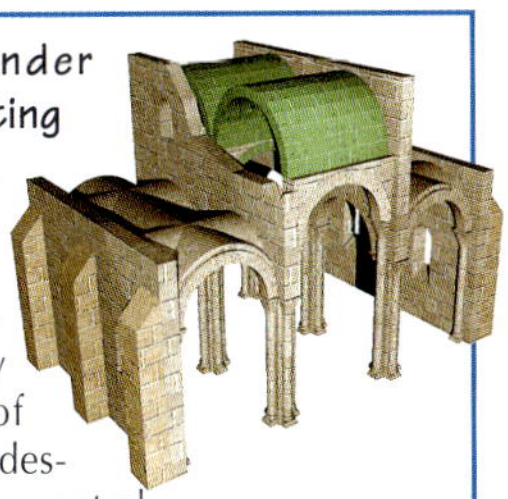

The oblique forces exerted by transversal barrel vaults cancel each other. It therefore becomes possible to open clerestory windows. But a row of transversal barrel vaults destroys the harmony of the central aisle.

❸ central aisle under pointed barrel vaulting

The pointed* arch is often seen as belonging only to Gothic* architecture. But it was already used during the Romanesque period (Burgundy, Provence etc.). Pointed* barrel vaults exert weaker oblique forces than the semi-circular vaults, the piercing of clerestory* windows was thus possible.

❹ church with a line of domes

There are few examples of this type of construction, perhaps influenced by Byzantine churches (☛ insert p. 9) in France (Perigueux, Cahors, Souillac, etc.). Its stability allowed the central aisle to be considerably widened (approx. twenty metres)... but because it was necessary to shoulder* the domes, no side aisles could be added.

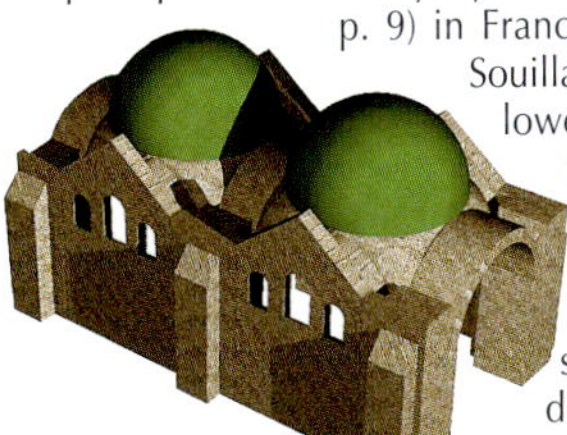

MAIN TERMS

→ : oblique force → : thrust → : load → : shouldering

EQUILIBRIUM. Equality of force between several opposing bodies, state of inertia of what is subjected to such forces.

FORCE. Any cause able to displace a body or able to deform it.

LOAD. Vertical force exerted by the weight of the upper parts of a construction on the lower parts.

OBLIQUE FORCE. Resulting from a load* and a thrust*. The more it tends to the vertical, the less it is effective.

THRUST. From Old Norse *thrysta*, "to press". Horizontal force.

TRIBUNE. From the Latin *tribunal*, semi-circular "platform" where the tribunes/magistrates sat (☛ APSE). A high gallery situated above a side aisle* having the same width (≠ TRIFORIUM, and LOFT, from Old English, *lyft*). By definition a tribune exists only in churches where the side aisles* have two levels (☛ SIDE AISLES, NAVE). It opens towards the interior of the church by a row of free openings* and towards the exterior by windows*. The main purpose of a tribune is not to allow easier circulation but to buttress* the oblique forces of the vault of the central aisle. In many Romanesque churches it provides one of the few ways of admitting light into the central aisle.

WEIGHT. Force due to terrestrial attraction (resulting from the laws of gravity) exerted on material masses. Weight, if it encounters no other forces is expressed as a load*.

AT THE HEART OF A ROMANESQUE CHURCH

"The [Romanesque] Church has three and sometimes five aisles. Thus it can take in the crowd which presses around it and creates order by imposing parallel paths on this surging mass."

Henri Focillon, *Western Ar*

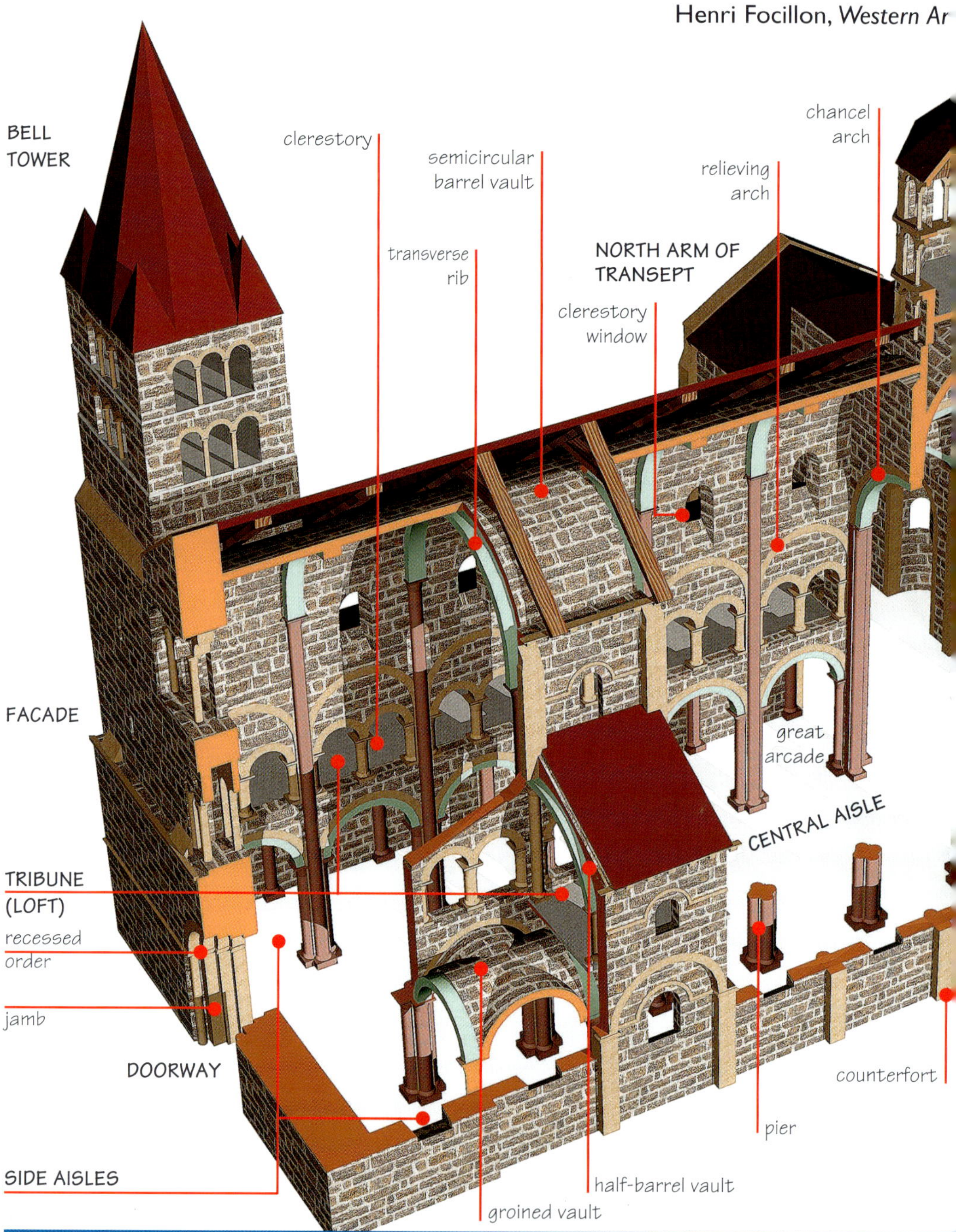

ROMANESQUE ART AND THE FEUDAL UNIVERSE

"And he [Jacob] dreamed and behold a ladder set up on the earth and the top of it reached the heaven, and behold the angels of the Lord ascending and descending it. And behold the Lord stood above it."

Bible, Genesis, Ch. 28, v 14 & 15 (Authorized Version).

Since the IXth century and the collapse of Carolingian* power, Western Europe, with the exception of the Holy Roman Empire, had been split up into a multitude of small territories held by men whose ties of vassalage and homage were the foundation of feudalism. In this universe divided and fragmented into a quantity of fiefs where every little overlord had power of life or death, the clerics — and religion — attempted to take the place of a declining royal authority and to appear as the sole safeguards of a higher law, of a universal order; this was the objective of a real institution, that of the "peace of God" for which the clerics would go as far as to arm militia. The clergy itself became feudal, especially that living "in the world" (priests and bishops) — as opposed to the monastic orders, which, inasmuch as the Barbarian invasions had allowed, remained cloistered as if separated from the world. The Orders started to reorganize around "mother" abbeys such as Cluny. In this economic, political as well as spiritual struggle which opposed them to the secular lords, the abbots* armed themselves with a God whom they proclaimed as the Lord of lords, so as to remind the secular lords that, facing their power, there existed an eternal hierarchy. The Romanesque "equilibrium", the purity and unity of its architecture were in fact the echo of that overwhelming, immanent, eternal feeling that the Church wished to represent in a dislocated world, of that order it wished to impose on feudality — and on the people. To a people who understood nothing of the Mass in Latin, the very order of architecture appeared as the best proof of the existence of an eternal order. Romanesque art, that strange mixture of serenity and anxiety : the monsters which covered the capitals* and which recalled the disorder reigning outside the house of God, the processions and the song, the long pilgrimages and the descent into the crypts where they could touch the relics with their own hands, formed for the faithful the framework of a spirituality inspired by the fear of the everlasting Judge and Lord.

Crypt of St. Seurin, Bordeaux. Viollet-le-Duc, Dict. Raisonné de l'Architecture.

Saint Étienne of Nevers, c. 1068 - c. 1097

Cluniac* Priory* Church, Saint Etienne has a classic plan. Its elevation nevertheless provides a perfect model, quite rare in Romanesque art: openings pierced directly under the vault of the central aisle above the tribunes light the nave despite the semi-circular barrel vaulting.

Overall length : 54 m.
Width of the central aisle : 7.80 m.
Height under the nave vault : 18 m.
Interior area : approx. 790 sq. m.

☛ plan page 6

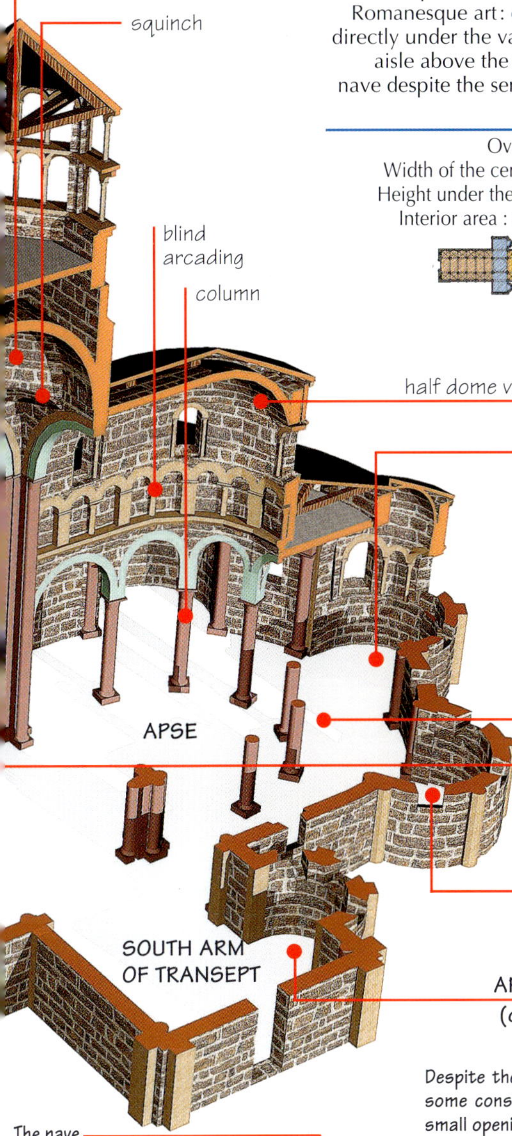

FACADES AND BELFRIES

Campanile: a bell tower free-standing from the church in the Italian tradition.

A belfry over the crossing of the transept.

Two belfries, one on each side of the transept.

Two belfries, one on each side of the chevet.

Harmonic facade.*

Porch belfry.

Wall-belfry.

Bellcote.

BELL (O.E. *belle*). Probably brought to the continent by the Irish monks. Their use became widespread throughout Europe during the Carolingian* period.

BELFRY. Tall construction meant to house bells. Its position in relation to the church can be varied .

A STRUGGLE FOR EQUILIBRIUM*

Despite the diversity of the Romanesque* buildings, the processes used had some constants: the narrow span* of the central aisle, thick walls, few and small openings (very often splayed* to make up for the lack of light), juxtaposition of mutually balancing volumes, the use of several sorts of vaulting within the same building... The essential part of the forces is contained and resolved inside the building: a Romanesque basilica differs from former buildings, not only because it is vaulted, but because its vaulting — being applied to a longitudinal building — needs the presence of a whole body of elements forming a structure able to cancel the forces exerted. This active structure becomes preponderant facing only passive structures (the supports). It would finally be prevalent during the Gothic* period.

The nave

All the constituent elements of a Romanesque* nave* are arranged so as to counter the oblique forces of the central aisle*; the nave is the key of the system. The solutions adopted for its covering determine the sort of edifice: ☛ page 15.

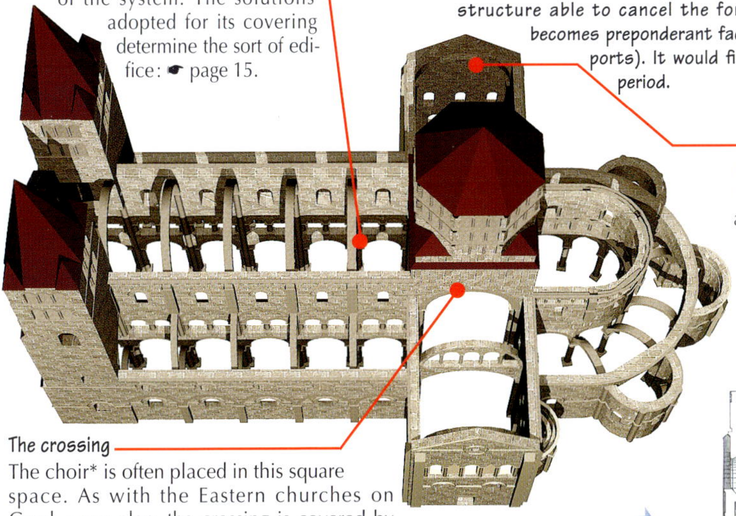

The transept*

It shoulders all the building and not only the crossing*, lights it from the sides and allows the faithful better entrances to and exits from the building by the arrangement of side doorways.

The crossing

The choir* is often placed in this square space. As with the Eastern churches on Greek cross plan, the crossing is covered by a dome on square plan, shouldered (when the church is oriented*) to the West by the nave*, to the East by the apse and to the North and the South by the arms* of the transept*. The weight of the belfry* which surmounts the dome constitutes an increase of the loads*, useful here to reduce the oblique* forces of the dome, thus adding to the equilibrium of the edifice.

Cross section of N. D. du Port, Clermont Ferrand, level with the transept: its barrel vaults shoulder **half-barrel* vaults buttressing*** the thrusts of the dome. Viollet-le-Duc. Op. cit.*

THE FORCES - GOTHIC LIGHT

The solutions brought to the problems of forces by Gothic architecture were linked to the systematic adoption of a new type of covering, cross-rib vaulting and to a new type of buttressing, flying buttresses. The mastery of forces became such that walls had much less importance and gave way to... light (☛ insert page 21).

❶ *The builders of the Gothic* period retained only two of the many solutions imagined by the builders of the Romanesque period.*

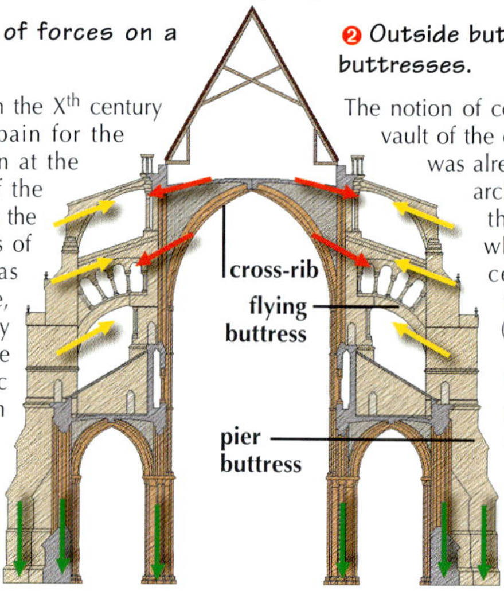

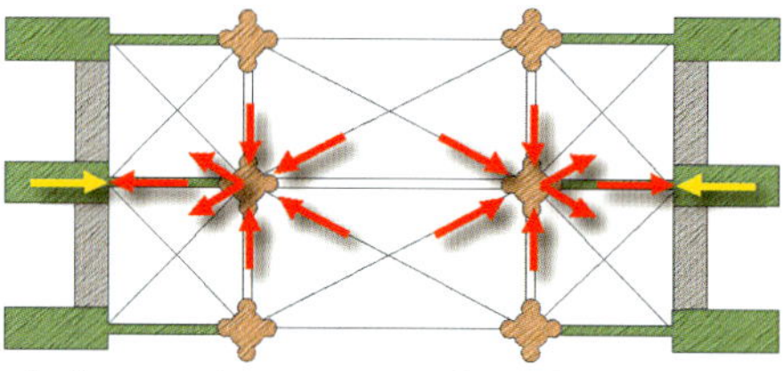

❶ Maximum concentration of forces on a precise point : ribbed* vaults.

Outlined by the Romans, used in the Xth century by the Muslim architects in Spain for the construction of domes and seen at the same period in the covering of the vaults of the churches in Armenia the cut stone supporting ribs*, kinds of bands of stone which serve as diagonals supporting a structure, already appeared, but only sporadically, in Romanesque architecture (porch of Moissac abbey church). It was in Durham Cathedral, begun before 1100, that Norman architects first used in a systematic fashion this method soon to be known as "cross-rib vaulting" which would see its triumph at Saint Denis.

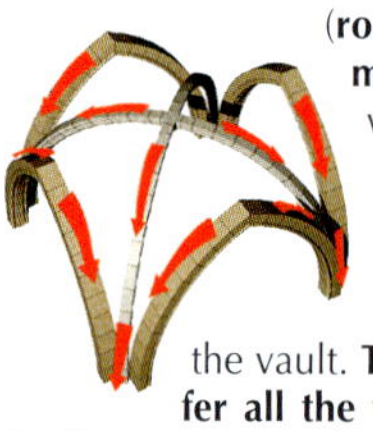

The cross*-ribs are arches (**round mostly**) which cross diagonally at the crown of the vault. **Their principal advantage is to transfer all the weight of the centre of the vault to its four supports**; because of their lightness, on the one hand they can span wide spaces (certain Gothic* vaults have a span* of more than 20 metres), but they also allow for large openings: in the first decades of the XIIth century, the pointed arch was chosen in place of the round arch for the arches flanking the four sides of the crossing (transverse* ribs and wall* arches) because on one hand the pointed arch effects a more efficient transfer, but also openings* under the wall* arches could reach as high as the keystone.

❷ Outside buttressing of the forces : flying* buttresses.

The notion of countering the outward thrust of the vault of the central aisle by an opposing thrust* was already largely present in Romanesque architecture. It was the part played by the half-barrels* of the tribunes*, which buttressed* the vault of the central aisle, frequently along **the whole length of the nave** (☛ page 14).

The appearance of ribbed* vaulting made it possible to counter the oblique forces at precise points: the combined effect of all the forces at the crossing of two ribbed vaults (in red in the opposite illustration) generates a single force. If on this precise point a counter-thrust is applied (in yellow) the outward thrusts are contained and their weight transferred to the supports. This possibility (and indeed, necessity) of strengthening the walls from point to point led to the appearance as early as the XIIth century of walls* buttresses which shoulder the central aisle. The builders rapidly realised that in this way they could make the building considerably higher. The idea was the following : to apply the system of the Romanesque half-barrels **but only at the points** where the thrust resulting from the forces of the cross-ribs was operative. This was the principle of the **flying buttresses**. A buttress reaching now as high as the central vault was imagined: this was the pier* buttress. Between the latter and the vault, the arches (the buttresses which "push") contain the outward thrusts and transfer them to their supports. This is a fundamental principle of Gothic architecture : **unlike Romanesque architecture, the neutralisation of the thrusts is no longer effected from inside the building but from outside.**

❷ *The Gothic church is no longer an edifice but a structure where the mastery of forces is embodied in stone.*

No more walls but great glazed openings, separated by a network of forces*. The determined and more frequent use of cut stone made possible the intricate chisel-work of the building in this way. The role of the material and the techniques of construction used were fundamental and each stone was now cut according to a given size (☛ p. 33). It was in that way and in that way only, course* after course, horizontal layer after horizontal layer, that an immense network of ribs might be built in which each one seemed to be erected independently from the construction. Arches, single banded in the Romanesque period, and columns were now covered with **ribs***, each of which seemed to conduct a particular force from the crown of the building to its base. This multiplication of ribs was not always necessary but underlined the rivalry between the edifice and weight, the genius of the master builders, the stone cutters and the masons.

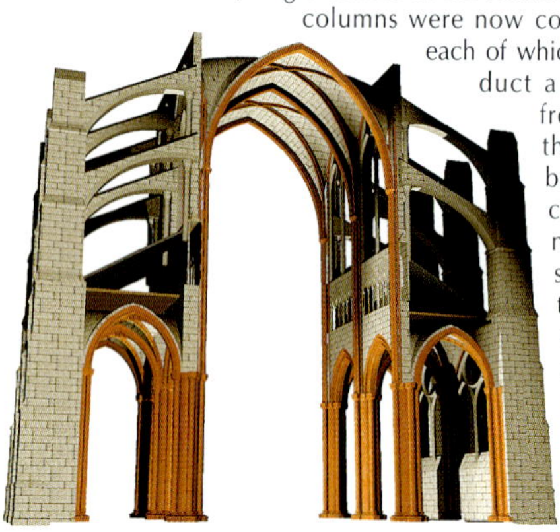

THE USE OF IRON

During the Gothic period stay* rods appeared in many constructions, these were a sort of iron tie beam which by joining the springings of the vaults or the flying buttresses one to another kept them in place. Iron bars could also be used to strengthen the stone ribs*, the diagonal ribs, the windows* or the rose* windows or to surround all or part of the edifice within the masonry (chevet of Notre Dame of Paris) even to constitute a real frame. This use of iron emphasizes the will of the Gothic builders to free themselves from an architecture in which the solidity of a building depended essentially on its weight, and on the resistance of the materials to the forces of compression. This will would one day be expressed in a totally different way by the use of steel, in the XIXth century.

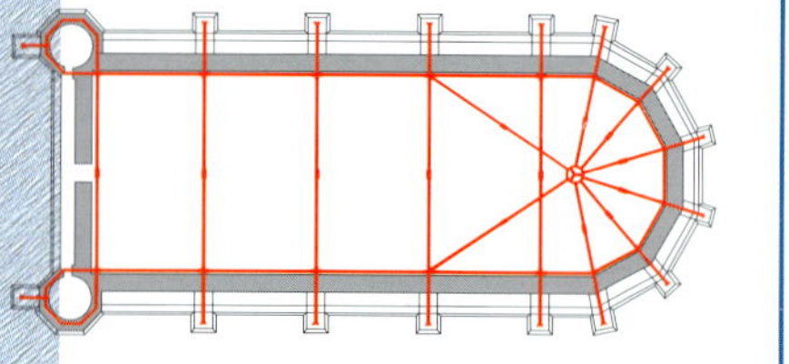

Metallic structure of the roof space over the vaults of the Sainte Chapelle, built by Saint Louis, Paris, c. 1240.

❸ *The slow disappearance of the tribune, so important in the Romanesque period... making way for the triforium which itself would soon disappear... All this can be interpreted otherwise : light always more light.*

Notre Dame of Paris, c. 1160 - c. 1200 (first phase)

The nave was already thirty-three metres high. But of these thirty-three metres a large part of the shell was still taken up by walls or rather by "panelling" which impeded light. The continuing presence of tribunes* (in red) forced the builders to vault them in an unusual way, in order to allow in as much light as possible. To let in more light, builders had to do away with the tribune.

Notre Dame of Chartres, 1195-1210 (for the nave)

Since the appearance of flying buttresses, there had no longer been any need for an internal buttressing. When the master builders realised this, the tribune disappeared and so the clerestory* windows could be made bigger. But there was still an impediment to the entrance of light: to the roof of the side aisle (in blue) there corresponded a blind surface in the central aisle. So that this surface might not remain empty and to give an impression of space, the triforium* appeared, a reminiscence of the tribune, it did not allow direct lighting but broke the monotony of a surface which could not otherwise be put to any use.

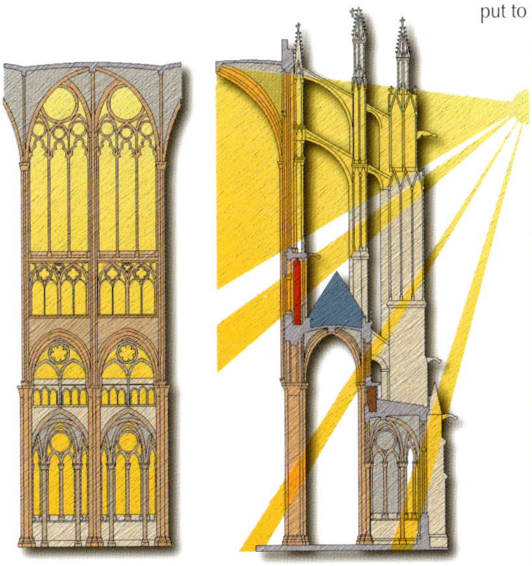

Saint-Pierre de Beauvais, 1225-1272

L'adoption d'un type de toiture pyramidal pour le bas-côté (☛ illust. ci-contre) permet de percer le mur aveugle du triforium et de l'ouvrir à la lumière. Les panneaux de remplissage ont pratiquement tous disparu au profit de la lumière, laissant de ce fait mieux apparaître la pureté de la structure, qui seule ou presque demeure. L'architecture gothique atteint son apogée (et ses limites : le chœur de Beauvais s'effondre en 1284 ; l'église ne sera jamais achevée). Si le vaisseau central n'a que quinze mètres de portée (à comparer avec les vingt-cinq mètres de la basilique civile de Maxence, ☛ page 4), il atteint une hauteur de plus de quarante-six mètres (quinze étages d'un immeuble moderne).

RAIN AND GARGOYLES...

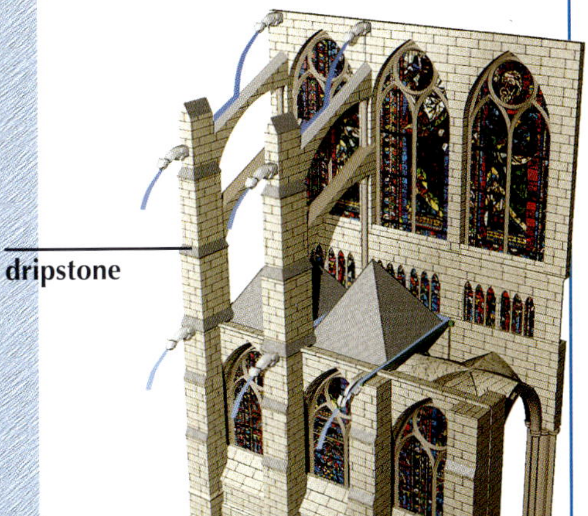

Water was conveyed away by gutters (stone channels) bordering the main roof and then was directed through gargoyles* to the gutters arranged at the top of the flying buttresses* to end up through the pier* buttresses in other gargoyles, whose purpose was to evacuate the water as far as possible from the foot of the walls. When the single pitched roof was no longer built over the side aisles*, it was necessarily replaced by a row of pyramidal-shaped roofs between which added gutters could be arranged conveying water to other gargoyles*.

MAIN TERMS

DRIPSTONE. Projecting moulding on a cornice, over a gutter to let water drip at a certain distance from the facings of a building. The dripstone of an opening often constituted an archivolt*.

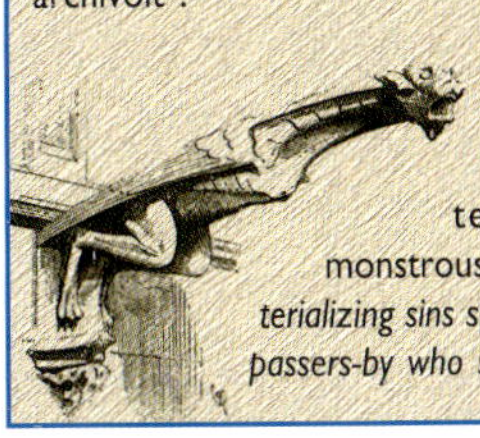

GARGOYLE. From low Latin *gurgulio*, "throat". Projecting spout by which rain water runs into gutters. Gargoyles are sculpted in monstrous shapes : *"these hybrid creatures materializing sins spouting from the sanctuary, reminding passers-by who see them spewing through their open mouths the scum of the gutters, that outside the bosom of the Church are found only obliquities of the spirit and iniquities of the soul."* (Huysmans, *la Cathédrale*).

STAY ROD. Horizontal piece of iron serving as a tie. Unlike stone which can not be subjected to forces of pressure, stay rods like wooden tie* beams can be subjected to such forces.

TRIFORIUM. From Low Latin *tres*, "three" and *foris*, "door". **1.** Narrow gallery situated over the side aisles or over the tribunes* and pierced by a row of openings. **2.** Sometimes designates the whole of the openings of a gallery or of a tribune overlooking the central aisle.

✔ AT THE HEART OF A GOTHIC CHURCH

"In the XIIth century the task of the religious establishments was accomplished; the monarchic powe[r] had grown, the civil order was trying out its strength and wanted to resolve itself into a body. It was a[t] this time that the episcopate undertook a work of reconstruction and rebuilt its cathedrals."

Eugène Viollet-le-Duc, *Dict. Raisonné de l'Architecture, art. cathédrale.*

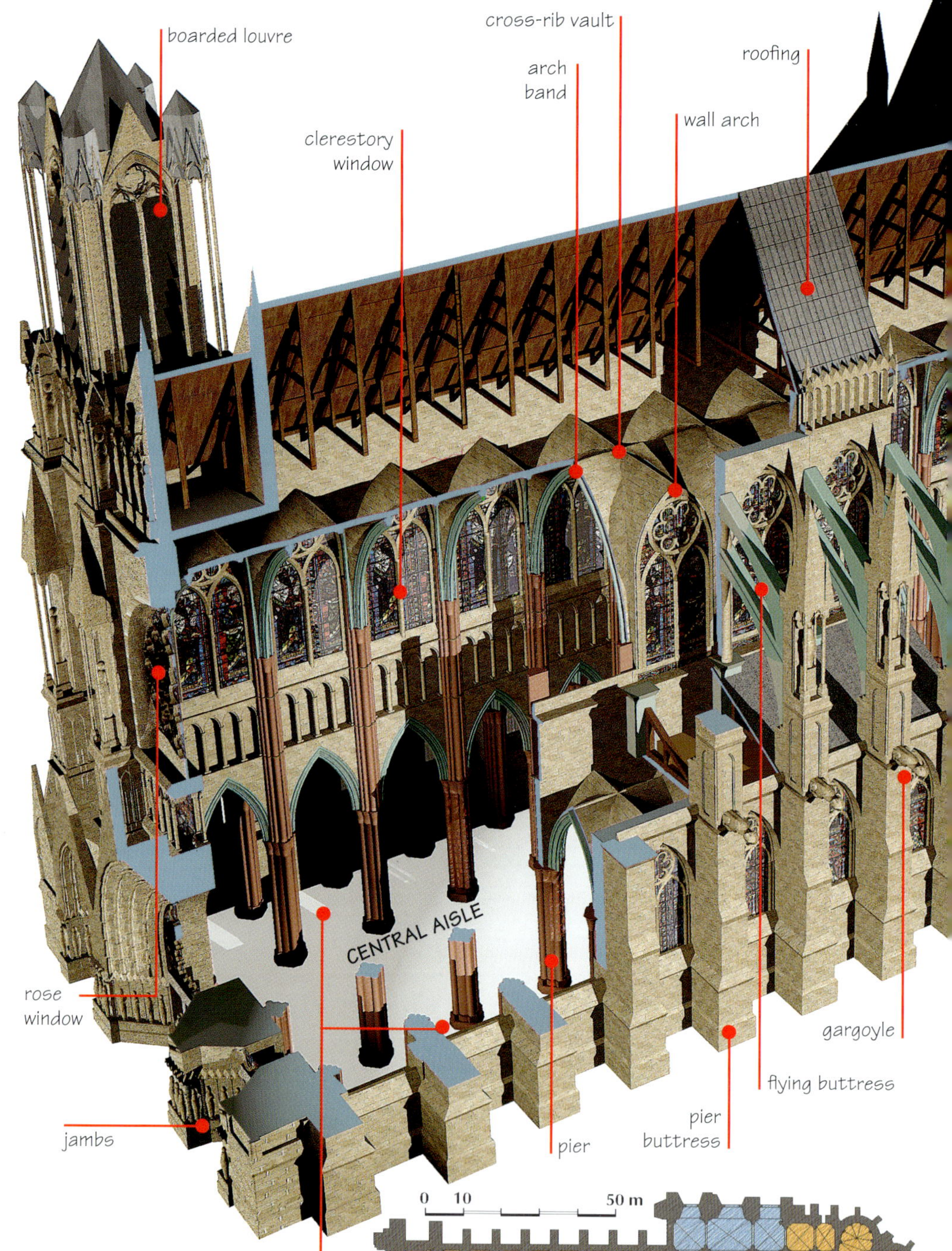

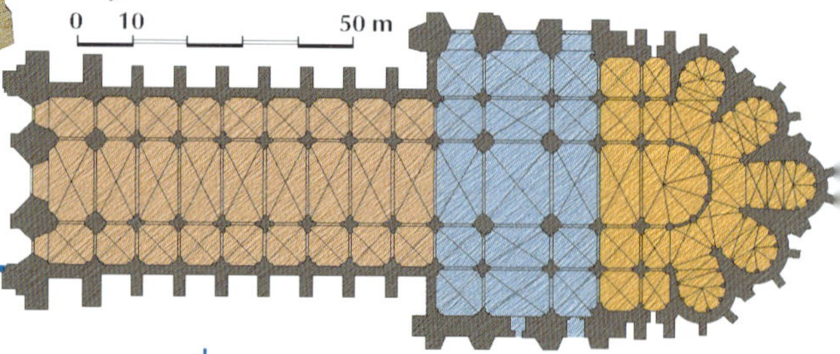

FACADE

PINNACLE. Crowning on square or polygonal plan ending in a cone or a pyramid.

ORNAMENTAL GABLE. Decorative triangular-shaped crowning often of open-work, surmounting an arch of an opening. A gable of this type is not therefore a roof gable*.

RHEIMS, *cathedral church where the Kings of France were anointed.*

Homogeneous, despite the successive intervention of four architects, it was erected between 1211 (on May 6th, Archbishop Aubry de Humber, who was the architect, laid the first stone) and 1286 (completion of the west facade). It marked the transition between the Classical Gothic* and the Rayonnant Gothic*. There appeared in this period, circa 1220, the stoneframe* window, used systematically in Rayonnant Gothic* style.

Overall length : 149.17 m. Length of the nave : 115 m. Height of the nave under the vaults : 38 m. Inside area : 4.800 sq. m.

Notre Dame of Rheims, 1211- c. 1260

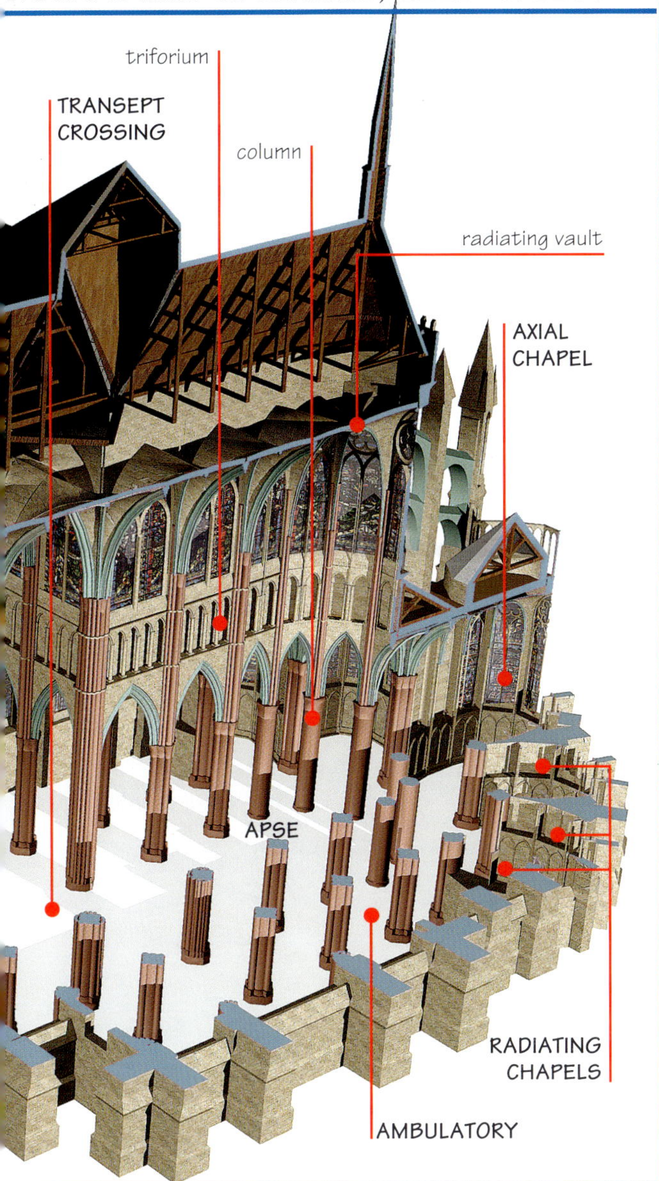

THE NORMAN INFLUENCE

Saint Etienne of Caen Late XIth century. Romanesque harmonic facade

Notre Dame of Paris Harmonic Gothic facade (1197-1208)

Anglo-Norman Romanesque art was determinant in the birth of Gothic architecture (as can be seen in the spread of ribbed vaulting introduced by the Norman architects at Durham ☛ §1 page 18). Already in the Romanesque period, the Norman builders created the **harmonic facade** built on a **ternary pattern**, marked **in elevation** (facade pierced with three levels of openings, these often joined in threes, the levels being separated by moulded string courses) **as well as on plan** (two symmetrical towers framing a central part, buttresses separating these three parts which each opened onto a gateway). To this original disposition, Gothic art adjoined a rose window, surmounting the central doorway and the outer galleries — such as the majestuous "gallery of kings" decorated with the statues of the kings and prophets of the Old Testament.

A THEOLOGY OF LIGHT.

"I am the light of the world; he that followeth me shall not walk in darkness, but shall have the light of life."
Gospel according St. John, VIII, 12 (Authorized version).

Technical innovations played a great part in the emergence of Gothic* architecture. But, from its very origins, willpower and one man would elevate this architecture to a veritable theological system. The work of rebuilding the abbey church of Saint Denis, the final resting-place of the Kings of France, began circa 1137. The man who conducted this work was himself abbot* of Saint Denis, his name was **Suger**. He was a childhood friend of Louis VI's and was ambassador to the Pope, and later one of the King's counsellors, before becoming advisor and minister to his son and successor Louis VII. The birth certificate of Gothic* architecture was signed when Suger asked the builders to open up the choir of Saint Denis to light by the use of cross-rib vaulting. By this using of certain architectural elements hitherto little used to serve a new idea, the abbot of Saint Denis was really imagining the edifice as a theological principle, a principle which he founded on anonymous writings attributed to Denys the Areopagite, confused with Saint Denis, the real patron of the abbey church. This theology rested on the idea that light was a divine manifestation or rather that *"God is Light"* and that every being received and transmitted that light according to a hierarchy devised by God. The stained* glass of the clerestory* windows of the Saint Denis choir were intended to confer to the abbey church the image of a celestial Jerusalem adorned with jewels. Suger had the holy reliquaries brought up out of the darkness of the crypts so that light could shine fully on them and the royal tombs (Louis VII himself carried up the relics of Saint Denis out of the crypt towards a new shrine set in the choir during the consecration of the latter). The divine light reflected from the gold and precious stones of this **treasure*** touched the clergy but also the faithful and the pilgrims... This light touched every man, and in this it was a kind of promise for every being. But light does not touch every man in the same way, and it was on that concept that reposed the divine hierarchy imagined by Suger, similar to the royal hierarchy he devised as a minister of Louis VII for a feudal society which he imagined as a pyramid, with the King at the summit. Suger's will was not a folly of alchemy or transcendence, nor was it only a theological will : it was at the same time a political will. Gothic* architecture was an architecture of royalty, invented in the Ile-de-France, in the royal domain and nourished by the new power — and riches — of the bishops, that is to say of the cities. Although born in an abbey, it was in the cathedral churches of the cities that it would grow (☛ page 22). The inordinate development of French cathedrals (the central aisle of Beauvais attains a height of forty-six metres under the vault) was the strongest expression of a common interest, that of a king relying on the emergence and emancipation of the parishes as opposed to feudality, of the bishops who, to ensure their own power, relied on the people, and the people of the towns who sanctified God and the king in order to acquire their own freedom.

Chapel of Rheims cathedral. Viollet-le-Duc, Dict. Raisonné de l'Architecture.

AN ENCLOSED WORLD

The fact that medieval churches were more often than not part of a more complex body is frequently forgotten because of their aspect and the interest aroused by their architecture. In fact from Romanesque abbbeys to the cathedral closes of the Gothic period it was a veritable network which surrounded the edifices of the Christian cult.

Places where monks* were gathered, the first western monasteries* were nothing more than enclosures assembling in a haphazard fashion huts around an oratory (from Latin *orare*, "to pray"). Progressively, however, these communities became more organized and more hierarchical. From the IXth cent., **abbeys** directed by an abbess or an **abbot** (from eccles. Greek *abba*, "father") developed following the Rule* of Saint Benedict. Abbeys were settled in the **rural areas** in contact with the real economic and political power, that of feudalism: soon becoming rich from the numerous donations made by lords and sovereigns and protected by the Papacy, until the XIIth cent. they would remain the sole centres for the conservation of learning — which often consisted only in the work of the copyists in the scriptoria*. In fact they were centres of development of religious architecture (☛ insert p. 16): the main Romanesque churches — including the churches in places of pilgrimage — were abbey churches.

Praying and working : the time-frame alloted to the monks for each of these duties needed a compact architecture organized fundamentally around **church*** and **cloister***. It was onto this cloister that opened rooms, each with a specific function determined by the life and activities of the community (☛ illust. below). Sometimes, in the larger abbeys, the lodgings of the lay* brothers as well as the infirmary and the novices'* lodging formed a kind of independent little monastery. The whole of the monastery was surrounded by an **boundary wall** or pale*. Near the gate, which itself had a lodging (the **gatehouse**), was the guest-hall intended to accommodate travellers. The abbot's lodging might also be situated there when it was not near the cloister. Also inside the main enclave were grouped the workshops which gave the monastery* an almost complete autonomy (bakery, laundry, smithy, etc.). The wealth of the monastery, however, came from the revenues drawn from its possessions. It was this monastic wealth — caricatured early on in the figure of the fat-bellied monk — which undermined the credibility of the abbeys. While the monastic orders were being destabilized, the **towns** were now **undergoing a revival**: taking advantage of the wealth arising from the most important surge of urban development known since ancient times, the bishops became the dominant figures of the Catholic religion. Directed by the **bishops***, the **cathedral close** underwent its own growth. It was generally enclosed by a rampart or by an unbroken row of buildings (episcopal palace, cathedral* church etc.). Within this enclosure, the organization was less strict than inside the monasteries. If the main element was, of course, the **cathedral**, the other buildings differed little from their secular counterparts : the bishop's palace was essentially a lordly dwelling and the **canons'*** houses differed from lay houses only inasmuch as there were no shops on the ground level. The cloister, often absent or built belatedly, held only a symbolic role. The few communal halls (chapter* house, refectory etc.) were often assembled in a single building, a "**common house**". Because of the pressure arising from the new demands for learning, intellectual activity became more organized and institutionalized. It was in the cathedral closes that **cathedral schools** were created and before long the first universities. It was also **this city within the town**, of necessity more open than the monastic world, which would become the site of the great architectural enterprises and of the **rise of the cathedrals***.

THE DIFFERENT PARTS OF A MONASTERY

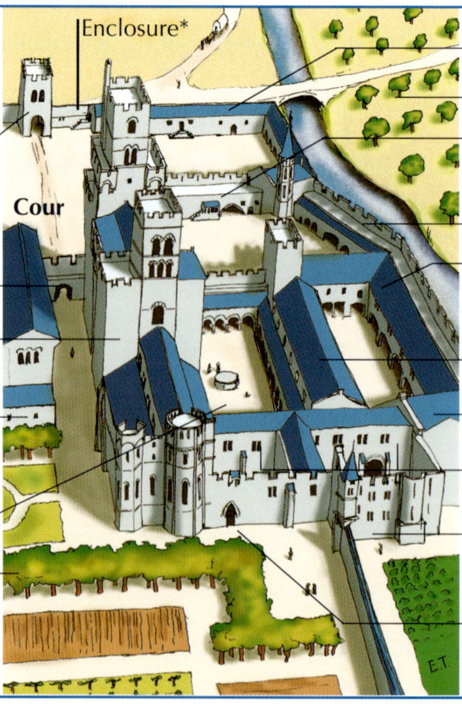

Abbey of Saint Allyre, Clermont-Ferrand, sketch by Éric Tranchart, adapted from Eugène Viollet-le-Duc.

MAIN TERMS

CHAPTER HOUSE. Room where the monastics assembled to begin every day with a reading from the Rule*. The arrangement of this room was the same as that of the liturgical choir*.

CLOISTER (from Latin *claustrum, claudere*, "to shut"). In a monastery* a square courtyard built on the model of the atrium* i.e. a garth bordered by a gallery (often vaulted from the middle of the XIIth cent.). Although at first intended to make circulation easier, the cloister soon became the heart of the monastery : the garth open to the sky, drew the eyes towards the heavens and so became a place for meditation and liturgy (processions etc.).

ENCLOSURE. 1. A wall or fence bounding an area subject to the particular jurisdiction of a monastery*. Lay people were not allowed inside this enclave. Also means the state of being enclosed in a religious community i.e. out of the secular world. **2.** ☛ p. 10.

MONASTERY. 1. Buildings where a community of monks* live, isolated from the world. **2.** The community itself.

SCRIPTORIA [sing. **SCRIPTORIUM**]. From Latin *scribere*, "to write". Room used for copying and illuminating, close to the library.

3

THE ELEMENTS

"And to and fro they go arguing about rib and arch."
Victor Hugo, *les Feuilles d'automne*, XXVIII.

ARCHES

To span an opening or a space, the architects of Ancient Greece used only lintel and architraves. Doubtless introduced into Rome by the Etruscans, arches woul progressively replace these former methods of construction to become the funda mental element of church architecture in the Middle Ages.

❶ *The primary role of an arch is to span a space and to deviate the forces* exerted.*

❶ The lintel

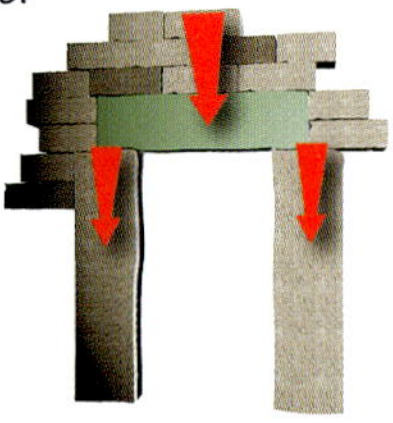

The simplest method of spanning a space is to place a stone — or lintel* — horizontally between two supports. But the transmission of forces* is in this case perpendicular to the superincumbent weight; the lintel is submitted to very great pressure and may split at its centre. It is impossible to span any wide space.

❷ The architrave

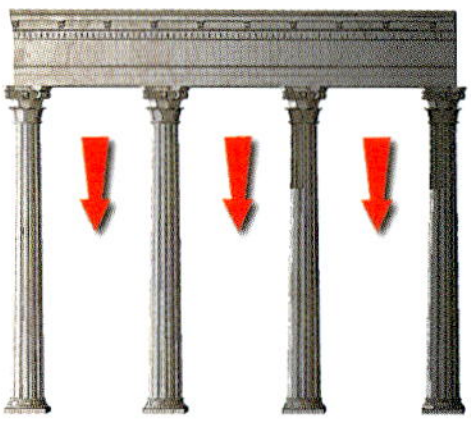

To span a wide space with lintels, the supports* must be multiplied. The ensemble of lintels is called the architrave*. As in the previous example, the elements are simply placed on their supports*.

❸ The arch

The arch was undoubtedly a major advance because it played a dynamic role : its shap allowed it to deviate the forces* generate by the superincumbent weight towards it supports*, which would allow for the ope ning of wider spaces notably between th columns (☛ insert page 14).

❷ *The arch is formed of independent elements wedged together, cut according to a specific angle.*

❶ unwedged arch

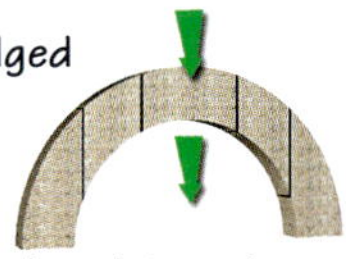

An unwedged* arch is made up of elements not held together by mutual pressure : it will collapse.

❷ corbel arch

A corbel arch (whose stones are arranged in horizontal corbel courses*) reacts like a lintel. It has the aspect and inner curve of an arch, but not its capacities.

❸ monolithic arch (arch in a single piece)

Theoretically it transmits to its supports the whole of the pressure it undergoes better than an arch with wedged* arch-stones. In practice, however, it was very rarely used because of the difficulty, indeed the impossibility, of finding stones large enough to be cut to this shape.

❹ wedged arch

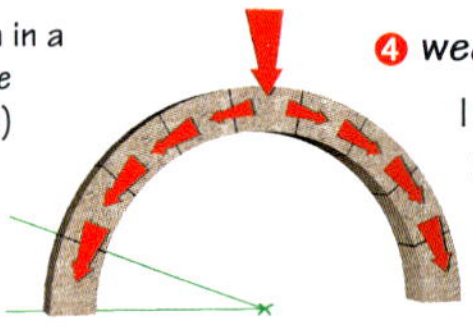

In fact most arches are made up of **several stones** which, cut **according to a specific angle, are held together by mutual pressure** : these stones are called **voussoirs*** (from low Latin *volvere*, "to roll", via French). If pressure is exerted on one of these stones it cannot break free and transmit that pressure to the neighbouring stones. This pressure being exerted laterally by irregular joints, the transfer of the weight to the supports is not absolutely vertical, a horizontal outward pressure is generated, the thrust*. Its role — of little consequence to the structure of an arch — is decisive to that of a vault (☛ pp. 14 to 17).

The construction of an arch needs a wooden scaffolding called a centring*.

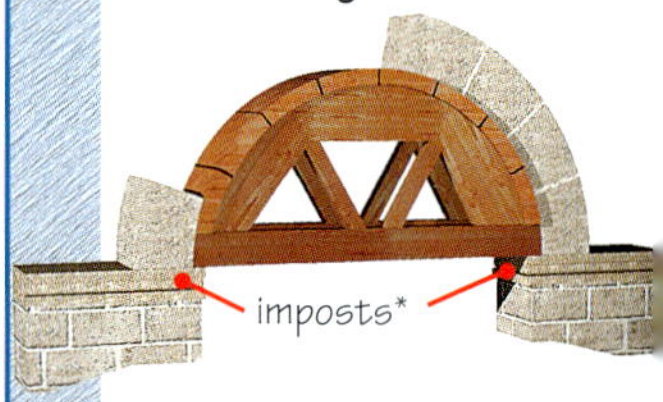

An arch made up of voussoirs* could not be built without scaffolding. But to avoid erecting a scaffolding along the whole height of the building, the supports of the arch were equipped at their summit with projecting stones, often carved, called **impost*** (or **abacus*** — from Greek *abax*, "a board" — in the case of piers or columns). These stones serve as supports for the **centring***. On this centring were placed the voussoirs or wedge*-shaped arch-stones forming the arch. The last to be set in place was the one in the centre, the keystone*, to block all the other stones of the arch, which was then said to be keyed up or locked, the centring could then be struck.

MAIN TERMS

ARCH. From Latin *arcus*, meaning a bow and later any object in the shape of a drawn bow. **1.** Curve formed by one or several portions of circles joined variously. **2.** Element of construction the profile of which was nearly always that of a curve but whose fundamental characteristic was to be made up of wedge*-shaped stones, elements held together by mutual pressure. ☛ VOUSSOIR*.

ARCHITRAVE. From the Greek *archos*, "principal" and Latin *trabis*, "beam". A series of lintels* resting on vertical supports.

CENTRING. Falsework made of timber upholding the voussoirs during the construction of an arch or a vault.

FLAT ARCH. Horizontal assemblage of several wedged elements set between two supports*. ☛ illust. insert p. 25. ✔ *It is an improved lintel, intended primarily as decoration.* ☛ PORTAL*.

LINTEL. From late Latin *limitaris*, "threshold, border", via Old French. Horizontal stone slab set across a space resting on two supports*. The underside of a lintel is called the soffit. ☛ LINTEL COURSE.

POINTED ARCH. Arch whose underside curve is made up of two segments of a circle forming two concave ribs joining at the summit; the **equilateral arch** (or three-pointed arch) is obtained by drawing two equal circles, the centre of the second is positioned on the circumference of the first. ✔ *The pointed arch, too often associated with Gothic* architecture, was already used in Romanesque* architecture.*

RELIEVING ARCH. An arch placed in a wall above a true arch or lintel to relieve it of some of the load and thrust.

ROLL. When an arch has two rows of superposed voussoirs* it is said to be a **DOUBLE ROLL ARCH**.

ROUND ARCH. Arch whose underside curve (the intrados*) forms a semicircle having its centre on the springing line. ✔ *The first of the arches from which all the others are derived, the round or semicircular arch was systematically used in Rome for civil architecture (bridges, aqueducts, amphitheatres, thermae, basilicas*, etc.) is today symbolic of Romanesque architecture. It remains however fundamental in Gothic* architecture in intersecting ribs* where the diagonal is, more often than not, a round arch.* ☛ POINTED ARCH, DIAGONAL* RIB.

WEDGE [to]. To set in place elements which would hold together by mutual pressure. ☛ VOUSSOIR*.

THE MAIN TYPES OF ARCHES

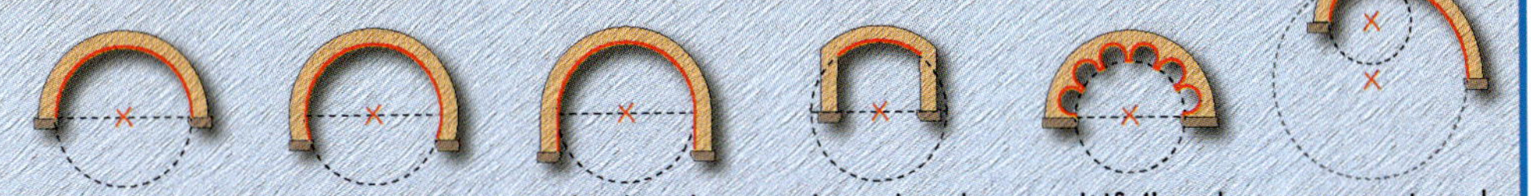

The different types of pointed arches are all derived from round arches

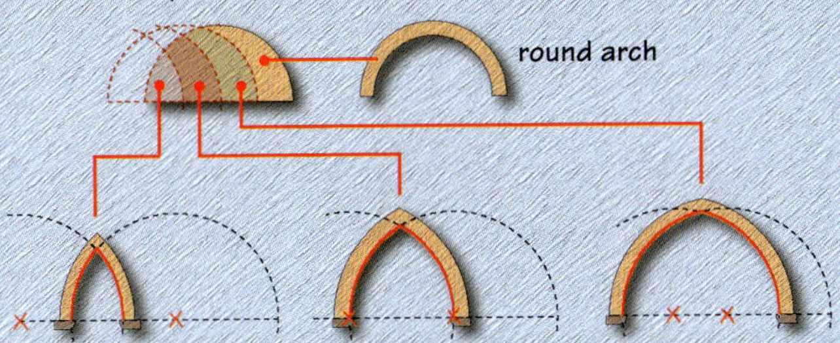

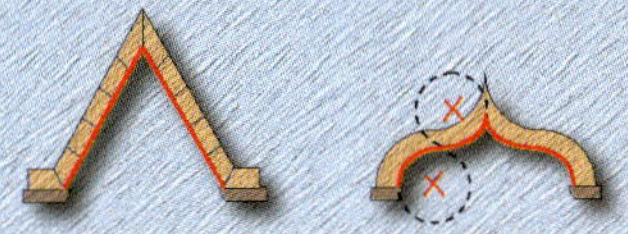

The flat arch is a borderline example: by its flat lower surface (or soffit) it can be considered as a lintel. But because of its wedged* elements, it is close to being an arch.

❸ *The fundamental arches are the round arch and the pointed arch*

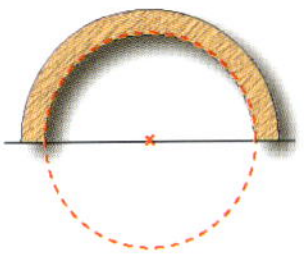

The intrados* of the arch is always a semicircle.

❶ The round arch

From the XIth century, the round arch was the main type of arch used in Europe (with its simplest derivatives, ☛ insert above).

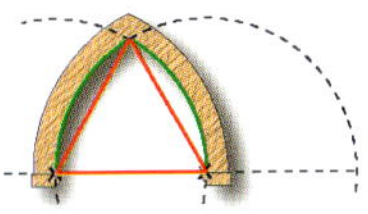

The equilateral or three-pointed arch is obtained by tracing a "third point" which forms with the first two an equilateral triangle.

❷ The pointed arch

The pointed arch, present in Syria and Armenia from the Xth cent. on, was doubtlessly brought back to Europe at the time of the Crusades. It has a great number of advantages over the round arch (☛ insert opposite).

THE ADVANTAGES OF A POINTED ARCH

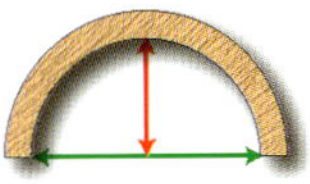

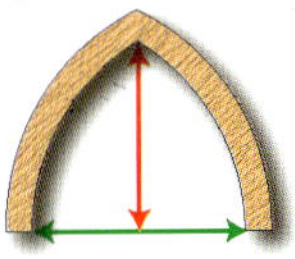

❶ A better transferring of forces

The ratio between the height and the span of a semicircular arch is always identical whatever its size: its rise — equal to its radius (in red) — is always half its span which is equal to its diameter (in yellow). In the case of a pointed arch, the ratio between the rise and the span decreases, it is even reversed (☛ lancet arch): the curves of the pointed arch are almost vertical; the outward thrusts* are less strong and the ratio between the load and the supports* more effective.

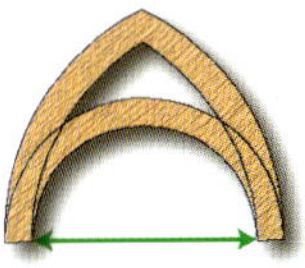

❷ A greater opening for light

For an equal span*, a pointed arch has a larger opening than a round arch. It therefore allows for larger windows.

RISE. The distance measured vertically between the centre of the span* of an arch or a vault and the apex of the intrados*.

SPAN. Horizontal distance measured between the two points of support of a lintel*, a timber* roof, an arch or a vault*.

❹ *An arch has a different name according to its function or its place in the structure.*

❶ to deviate the forces

The **relieving arch** can strengthen a wall or allow for the opening of a window.

❷ to uphold a vault

this is called the **transverse*** **arch**, ☛ § 4 p. 15.

❸ to buttress*

this is the function of the **flying*** **buttress** ☛ § 1 p. 18.

❹ to deviate & support

this is the role of the **diagonal*** **arch**. ☛ § 1 p. 18

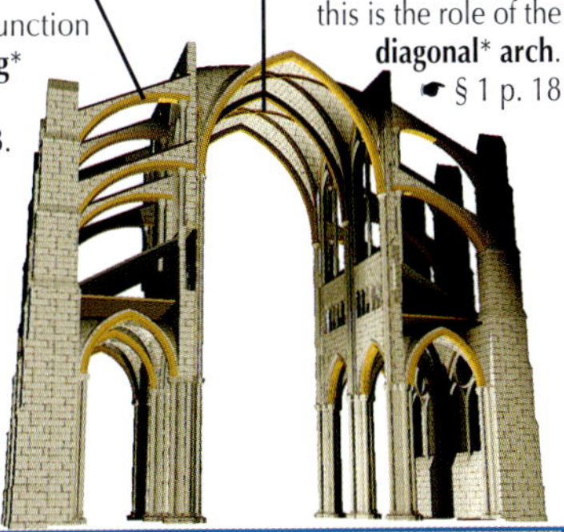

ELEMENTS OF AN ARCH

CONTACT FACE. Surface by which a voussoir* enters into contact with another voussoir. It is this face which receives and transfers the pressures.

EXTRADOS. External surface of an arch or vault.

IMPOST. Projecting horizontal block crowning a vertical support without a capital on which the springers of an arch rest. The impost plays an important part during the construction of an arch: it is used as a support for the centring* (☛ insert preceding page).

INTRADOS. The under surface of an arch or vault.

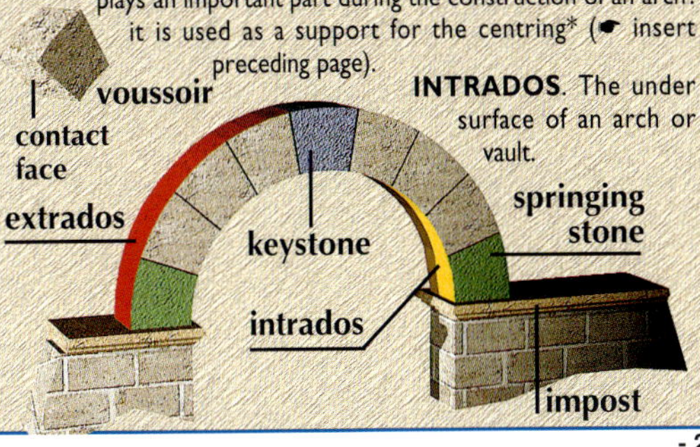

KEYSTONE. From Old English *ceg* and *stàn*. The stone at the apex of an arch, a flat arch or a vault. In spite of being the last stone to be set in place so as to lock the whole, it has no special function except that it is the one often sculpted.

SPRINGER. In an arch or vault, the first voussoirs or row of voussoirs laid without the use of the centring. The body of voussoirs* whose centre of gravity rests directly above the support of the arch.

SPRINGING POINT. The point at which an arch or vault rises from its support.

SPRINGING STONE. The first voussoir on either side of an arch or a vault. Its bottom contact face is horizontal and its upper face oblique to enable it to wedge the following voussoir.

VOUSSOIR. From Low Latin *volutis, volvere*, "to roll" via French. A wedge-shaped stone used in building an arch or a vault or a flat arch. The arch-stones are cut in such a way as to block each other mutually once set in place because of their wedge shape, the intrados* and extrados* are both curved: ☛ FLAT ARCH.

VAULTS

Favoured by Romanesque and Gothic* builders, the cut* stone vault dominatec the whole of medieval architecture. From the end of the XIth century, however, i underwent a major evolution, becoming a system of converging forces* thanks tc its stone ribs.*

❶ *Whilst the Romans frequently used the method of concrete vaulting, the use o vaults built of blocks of cut* stone became general during the Middle Ages.*

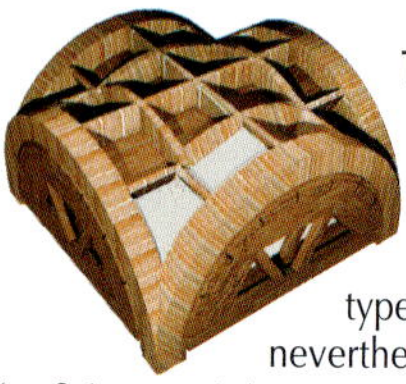

THE CONCRETE VAULT is a monolithic block, made by pouring concrete onto a centring* in brick forms. This was a method widely used by the Romans (☛ illustration page 4). This type of vault offered great stability. It was, nevertheless, rejected by medieval craftsmen (☛ § 1, page 14).

THE CUT* STONE VAULT is ar **assemblage** of **voussoirs***, stones cu in wedge shape, which allow it, like the arch*, to transmit its weight to wards its points of support. It is much lighter than the concrete vault but gene rates considerable pressure by its lateral thrusts (☛ §1, p.14) Furthermore, a centring* is needed for its construction.

❷ *Romanesque vaults were each adapted to a particular type of volume.*

❶ Domical

(or hemispherical vault), this is most certainly the oldest type of vaulting. During the Romanesque period it was the ideal method for covering a **transept crossing** : on the one hand because it made easy the vaulting of large square spaces and on the other because the other vaults could shoulder* it at its four sides at this point (☛ p. 17). It was also used in churches with a line of domes (☛ illust. n° 4 p. 15) and in the East as the central vault of churches built on Greek-cross plan (☛ insert p. 9).

The only real difficulty engendered by the dome comes from its connection to a square base. Two different systems enable this connection.

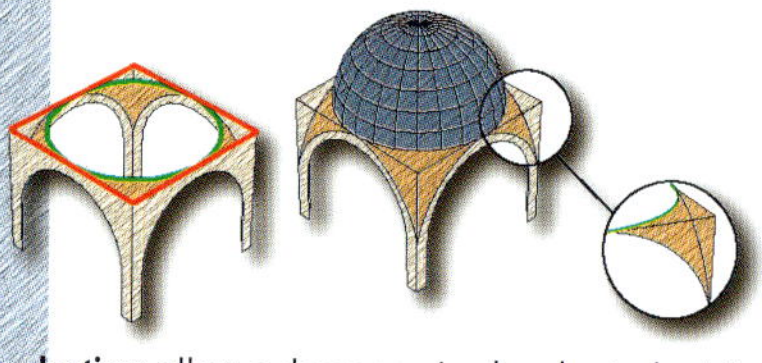

Pendentives allow a dome on circular plan to be joined directly onto a square plan.

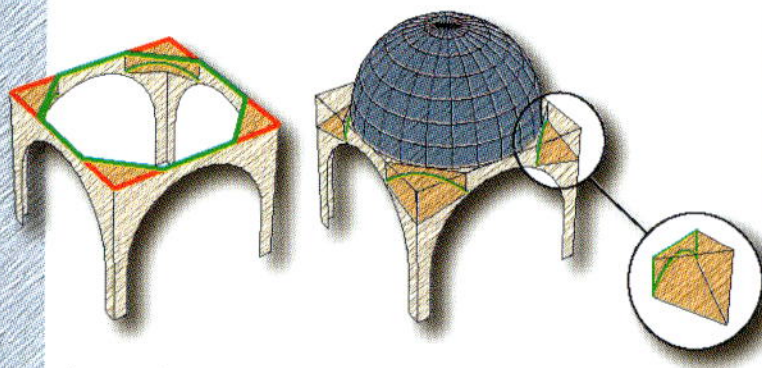

Squinches : the square is transformed into an octagon by four squinches placed on its angles. Unlike the pendentives, however, the squinches do not completely fit the circular shape of the vault.

❷ Half-domical (or semi-cupola vault)

From the time of the civil basilicas* of Rome (☛ § 2 p. 7) until the end of the Romanesque period, this vault was the covering *par excellence* used for **apses*** and **apsidal* chapels**. The half-dome only exerts thrusts on the bearing wall and none on its open side.

❸ The semicylindrical barrel or tunnel vault

is the simplest way of covering the **central aisle*** of a nave. It has the great disadvantage, however, of exerting thrusts* along all the length of its bearing-walls (☛ illust. p. 14).

❹ The pointed barrel vault

is the only Romanesque vaul which did not exist in Roman times. Appearing in the early XIIth century, notably in Cistercian* architecture, the pointed* barrel vault brought the pointed arch into **Romanesque*** churches. The thrusts it exerts are not as great as those exerted by the semicylindrical kind (☛ insert p. 25).

❺ The penetration vault

allows cross vaults (lunettes*) to be opened directly in the vault... thus weakening it dangerously.

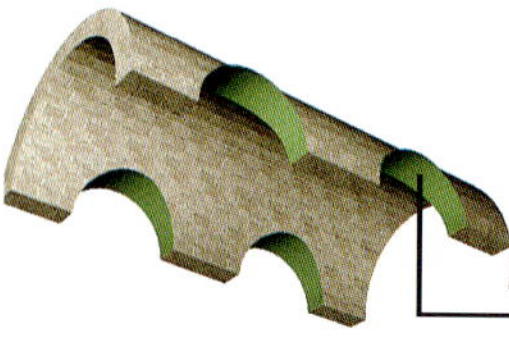

lunette*

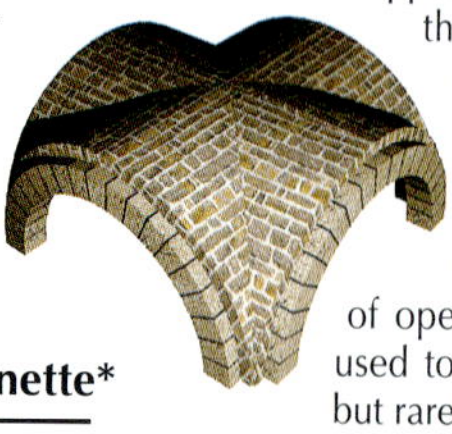

❻ The groin vault

appeared as early as the Roman era out of the will to open the flanks of a vault without weakening the structure (☛n° 5). It transmits part of its thrusts* towards particular points, thus freeing the lower spaces of the arches which support it, thereby allowing for the creation of openings. In Romanesque* architecture it was used to vault the **side aisles*** and the **ambulatory*** but rarely the central aisle (☛ p.15).

A groin vault fills schematically the crossing of two semi-cylindrical barrel vaults.

MAIN TERMS

BARREL VAULT. Vault whose alignment is given by an arch, and which is extended either following a straight line or a curve (an **ANNULAR VAULT** in an ambulatory*). By barrel vault it is generally understood **SEMICYLINDRICAL BARREL VAULT**, i.e. a vault following the curve of a round* or semicircular arch.

CROSS-RIB VAULT. Vault carried by at least four arches, two transverse* and two diagonal* (often also by two wall arches). It is **STELLAR** when it has liernes* and tiercerons* forming a star-shaped pattern, or **RADIATING** when the numerous diagonal ribs radiate around the keystone.

DOME (or cupola). From Latin *domus*, "home" via French *dôme*. Hemispherical vault.

GROIN VAULT. Vault composed of four cells or webs* which at their junction form jutting edges intersecting at a common crown. The groin vault is carried by four arches resting on four supports (☛ illust. insert page 14).

HALF-BARREL VAULT. Vault forming half-section of a barrel vault often covering a side aisle* or a tribune* and used to buttress* the vault over the central aisle (☛ § 4 p. 15).

PENETRATION VAULT. Barrel* vault intersected by transverse barrels called lunettes*.

POINTED BARREL VAULT. Barrel* vault following the curve of a pointed* arch.

VAULT. Middle English from low Latin *volvita*, "a roll", via Old French *voute*. Masonry work built on (and between) supports* and used to roof a volume.

❸ *Gothic* vaults were all built on the same system : that of ribs* of cut* stone.*

The ribs are pointed arches of cut stone whose purpose is to support the web of the vault during and after construction and to transmit its weight towards its supports.*

The simplest example of a rib vault is that of the quadripartite vault (☛ opposite) the main difference between this and the groin vault lies in the diagonals : two stone ribs* are placed under the groins to direct the entire weight of the vault towards particular points (☛ page 18). If the transverse* and wall* arches (which may be identical but which do not serve the same purpose) are always pointed* arches, the two fundamental ribs (the diagonal* ribs) are almost always **round arches**.

The ribs of the vault before the setting in place of the web

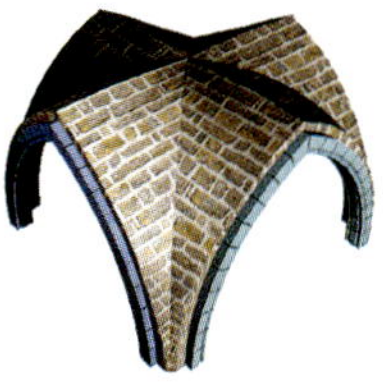

The finished rib vault

The conventional representation of types of covering* on a plan

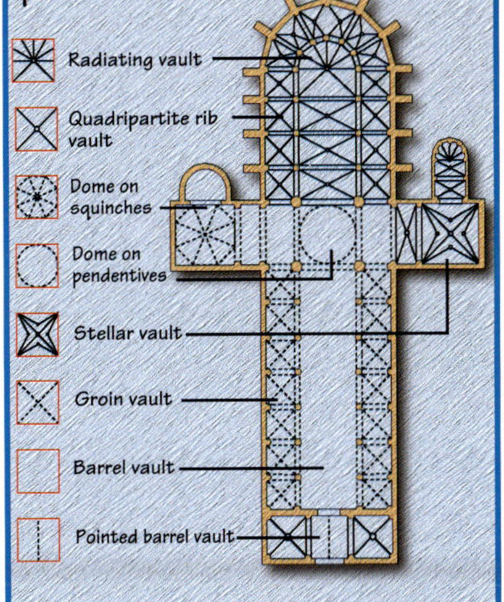

The ribs of cut* stone were adapted to each sort of volume

❶ Central and side aisles

QUADRIPARTITE vault (four diagonal ribs, two transverse* arches, two wall* arches).

SEXPARTITE vault (six diagonal ribs, two transverse arches, four wall arches : four openings).

QUADRIPARTITE on rectangular plan (☛ opposite, § 4). Covering of the central aisle.

❷ Transept crossing and apse

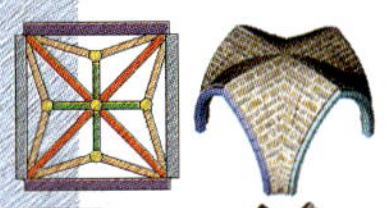

STELLAR VAULT. Usually covered the transept* crossing*. ☛ illust. insert below.

RADIATING VAULT. This replaced the Romanesque half*-dome vault to cover the apse*.

❹ *The intersecting ribs underwent an evolution linked to the height of the vault.*

The sexpartite vault has four wall arches and therefore four openings instead of two.

For the covering of the central aisle, the quadripartite ribbing* was rapidly abandoned by the master builders in favour of a vault reinforced by an added transversal rib : the **sexpartite** vault introduced into the nave a rhythm of strong and weak piers corresponding respectively to the springing of the diagonal and transversal ribs. But this vault was to disappear : like the quadripartite, its semicircular ribs, being situated in a rectangular plan, attained a height which forced the builders to raise to a dangerous level the walls flanking it which supported the timber frame roof. So the builders went back to a **quadripartite** vault but on **a rectangular plan** : its width equal to that of the central aisle, its ribs* having a reduced span — and therefore a reduced height. From the Classical Gothic* period on, this type of vault became prevalent.

Quadripartite vault on rectangular plan.

ELEMENTS OF A VAULT

DIAGONAL RIB. One of the two halves of a rib*, between support and keystone.

LUNETTE. From French, *lunette*, "little moon". Opening of a barrel vault in another vault of a larger radius called a penetration* vault.

PENDENTIVE. Support* in the shape of a concave triangle. ☛ insert p. 26.

QUARTER. ☛ WEB.

RIB. Moulded arch or segment of an arch, projecting at the intrados of a vault or forming the arch of an opening.

SQUINCH. Support* consisting of a diagonal arch and a small vault supporting the arch by corbelling. ☛ insert p. 26.

TRANSVERSE ARCH. Arch* stretching under a barrel vault or between two vaults to transmit a part of the weight of these vaults to its supports*. The space between two transverse arches corresponds generally to a bay*.

WALL ARCH. Arch stretching between two points of support of a groin vault or a cross rib vault and supporting these vaults lengthwise over a nave*.

✔ *A cross rib vault is carried (apart from the ribs themselves) by four arches which may be identical. The **transverse arches** which stretch perpendicularly to the nave are necessary. The **wall arches**, set along the length of the nave are optional, they are however often there, their intrados* forming the upper arch of the Gothic* openings.*

WEB [or CELL]. Part of the vault limited by groins (groin vault) or ribs (cross rib vault). Because the webs of groin vaults or quadripartite vaults are four in number, they are sometimes called QUARTERS.

Elements of a ribbed vault

DIAGONAL RIB. Stone rib* passing diagonally through the keystone* linking two points of support. Because the diagonal ribs cross at the keystone, the vault they carry is called a cross* rib vault. It is the diagonal ribs which transmit most of the weight of the vault to precise points and allow the cross rib vault to attain a span* (up to 20 metres) that the Romanesque groin vault had never been able to attain (not more than ten metres). Unlike the transverse* and wall* arches of a cross rib vault, diagonal ribs are mostly semicircular.

KEYSTONE. The last voussoir* set in place in the centre and at the crown of the ribs* of a ribbed vault. The keystone was often decorated.

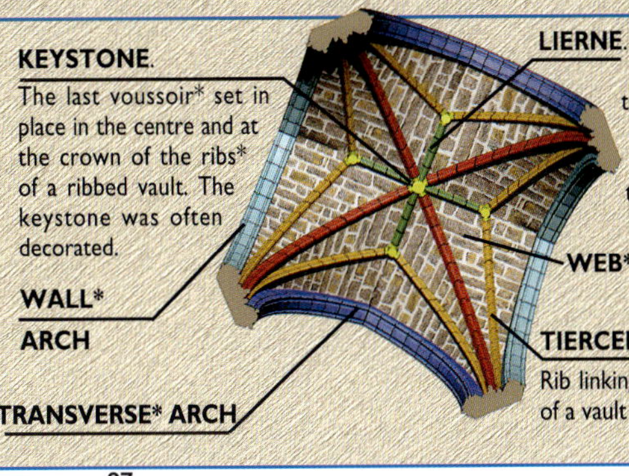

LIERNE. Rib which links the crown of a transverse arch, a wall arch or tiercerons* to the keystone of the vault.

TIERCERON. Rib linking the springing of a vault to a lierne.

TIMBER FRAME ROOFS

Wood does not behave like stone : whilst the latter can only resist forces of pres sure, wood is capable of resisting tensile and compressive stress. The history o timber frame roofs is that of a better use of these two forces*.*

❶ *The decisive innovation in timber frame roofs appeared earlier than Christiar churches : it was the invention of the truss*.*

Greek timber roof, arsenal at Piraeus, IVth cent. B.C.

The timber frame here acted like masonry : the pieces of timber rest one on the other and the whole was held in place simply by **piling**. The width of the central aisle depended on the length of the beam (in green) which, acting like a lintel*, could hardly exceed a span of ten metres.

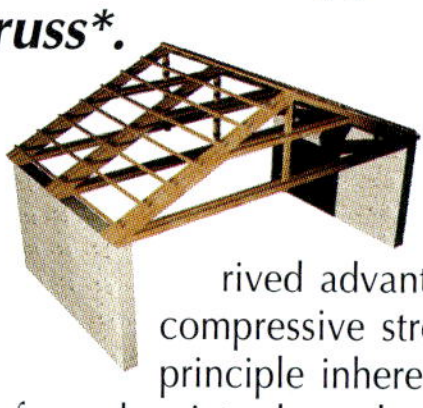

Roman tie beam roof

A Greek or Roman invention, the **roo truss*** (each of the triangles opposite) de rived advantage from the possibilities of tensile an compressive strength afforded by timber, similar to th principle inherent to the bow or crossbow : each truss formed an interdependent triangle consisting of two principal* **raf ters** (which, bending under the weight, could transfer their force to a horizontal piece, the tie* beam which acted like a stay* rod) Such a timber roof might attain a span of more than twenty metres

❷ *The appearance of stone vaults did not condemn the timber roof but forced it tc evolve.*

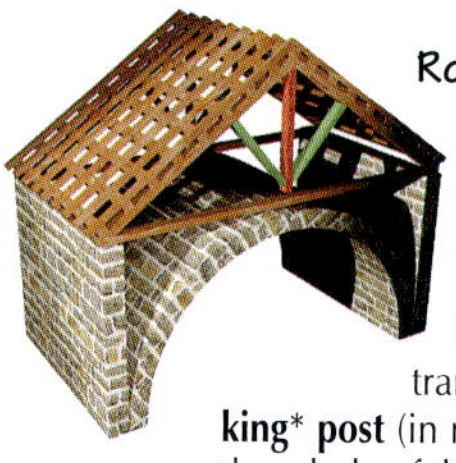

Romanesque timber roof, IX-XIIth cent.

During the Romanesque period, the whole of the roof formed a welcome increase in the load*, which "crushed" the oblique forces of the vault (☛ n° 5 of § 4 page 15). The use of **braces*** (in green) became widespread. By transmitting part of the load of the rafters to the **king*** **post** (in red), they relieved the tie* beam and stiffened the whole of the truss.

Romanesque timber roof with collar bean

Sometimes the tie* beam is not placec at the foot of the rafters* but higher up (it is then called **collar beam**) ir order to limit the height of the walls above the vault.

❸ *The Gothic period saw an increase in the use of trusses* and a general lightening of the structure.*

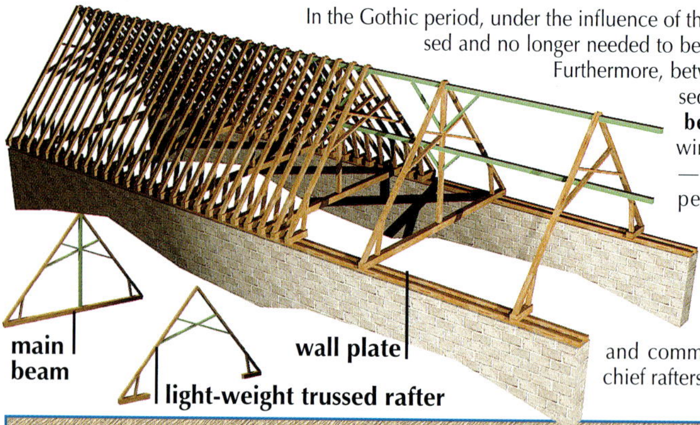

In the Gothic period, under the influence of the northern timber roofs, the braces* were crossed and no longer needed to be joined to a king post to relieve the tie* beam. Furthermore, between the principal trusses appeared an increased number of **intermediate trusses without tie* beams**, joined to the whole by a system of wind* braces (in green) and by another element — which did not exist in the Romanesque* period — the template (or wall plate). The ensemble was now more resistant and — to be noted for a period lacking wood — needed less large section lumber (☛ p. 32). Furthermore the increase in the number of trusses led to the disappearance of purlins* and common rafters* (☛ illust. below) which became chief rafters and directly supported the roofing.

MAIN TERMS

COVERING. Work limiting a space at the top (vault, if the edifice is vaulted, ceiling and even the timberwork if the edifice has neither vault nor ceiling).

LEAN-TO (ROOF). Roof with a single slope. ☛ illust. page 7.

ROOF-SPACE. Space between the slopes of a roof and a floor or a vault.

ROOFING. External surface protecting the edifice from bad weather. ✔ *Generally Romanesque* roofing is of stone slabs or tiles, Gothic* roofing is of slate or lead.*

SADDLEBACK ROOF. Roof with a double slope between two gables* (☛ illust. below & p. 7). Also called pitched or gabled roof.

TIMBERWORK ROOF. Pieces of timber assembled to form the skeleton of the roof. During the Romanesque* and Gothic* periods, timber frames were built before vaults (as protection and as scaffolding).

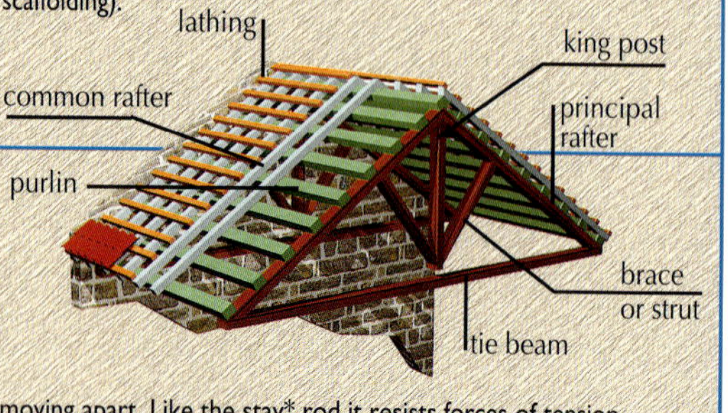

Elements of timber frame roofs

BRACE or **STRUT**. Oblique piece of a truss*, linking a king* post (often at its base) to a principal* rafter.

KING POST. Vertical post of a truss* at the joining of the principal* rafters at the middle of the tie* beam or carrying only the base of the braces* without resting on the tie beam.

LATHING. Body of laths of wood supporting a covering*.

PRINCIPAL RAFTER. Oblique beam of a truss* carrying either the purlins* (Romanesque and Gothic periods) or the lathing* (lattice) (Gothic period). In the latter case, it is a **CHIEF RAFTER**. The **COMMON RAFTER** is a length of timber joined onto the purlins and on the same slope as the principal rafters. It carries the lathing.

PURLIN. Post linking trusses together, carried by the principal* rafters and holding up the common rafters*.

TIE BEAM. Major horizontal beam at the base of a truss to which are fixed the lower ends of the rafters to prevent them moving apart. Like the stay* rod it resists forces of tension.

TRUSS. Middle English sense : *bundle* from late Latin *tors* via old French *trusse*. Triangular framework (in vertical plan and perpendicular to the length of the roof) generally made up of two rafters* and a tie* beam (sometimes of a king* post and/or braces*).

WALL PLATE (or TEMPLATE). Horizontal timber post resting on a wall and serving as a link between the bases and the trusses. ☛ illust. § 3.

WIND BRACE. Body of timber pieces which join together the trusses to prevent racking.

SUPPORTING MEMBERS

Supporting members are basically of two sorts : columns or piers. From the Romanesque period to the Gothic* period, inasmuch as the complexity of vaulting and stone ribbing increased, so of necessity did the complexity of the shape and form of supports.*

attached* column

❶ **the column** : its primary purpose is to support the springing of arches (and less frequently of vaults or walls) which surmount them and to transfer them to its base. **Columns are splayed at the top** (the capital) **and base** in order to improve the concentration of forces and to ground them.

❷ **the pier** which may be of varied composition (simple square member, a cluster of columns etc.) supports heavier loads* than the simple column. Its shape is often determined by its place in the church and the type of structure it must support : simple arches, double rolls etc. Relatively simple during the Romanesque period, it became more complex during the Gothic period in order to accept the numerous ribs of the cross rib vault (☛ insert below).

A few columns and piers

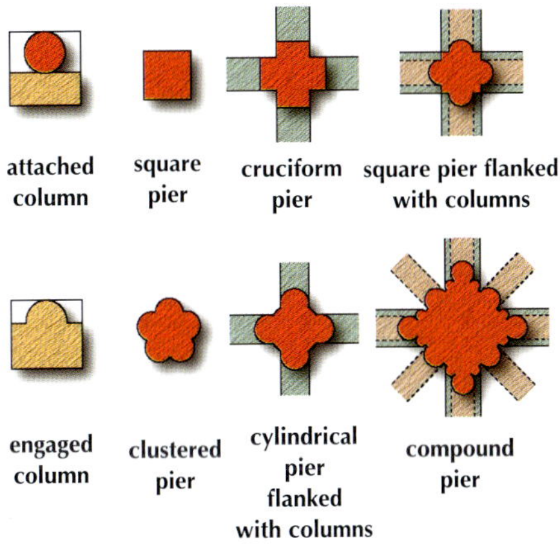

MAIN TERMS

COLONNADE. A line of columns and their covering (ancient architecture).

COLUMN. Support consisting of a vertical shaft (polygonal or circular) of a base and a capital. A column of small section is called a **COLONNETTE**. An **ENGAGED COLUMN** is one applied to or built onto a support*, projecting by half its diameter (generally hewn out of the same block as this support, it is not in the strict sense of the term a column). An **ATTACHED COLUMN** is one set against a support* but with only its capital and its base engaged in this support.

DOSSERET. A sort of pilaster without base or capital against which is applied a column or a pilaster.

PIER. Any support with the strict exception of a column or a wall (two coupled columns are in fact a pier). The simplest pier is on **RECTANGULAR PLAN**. A **CANTONED** pier is flanked by engaged columns. A **CLUSTERED** pier consists of a group of shafts, often coupled, around a more massive central core. ☛ illust. above.

PILASTER. Slightly projecting vertical support, usually rectangular in shape with base and/or capital and engaged in a wall.

SUPPORT. Any member which upholds, supports a load*. The main supporting members are the **wall**, the **column**, the **pier**. ✔ *The role of a support is to transmit any load* to its base.*

The elements of a column

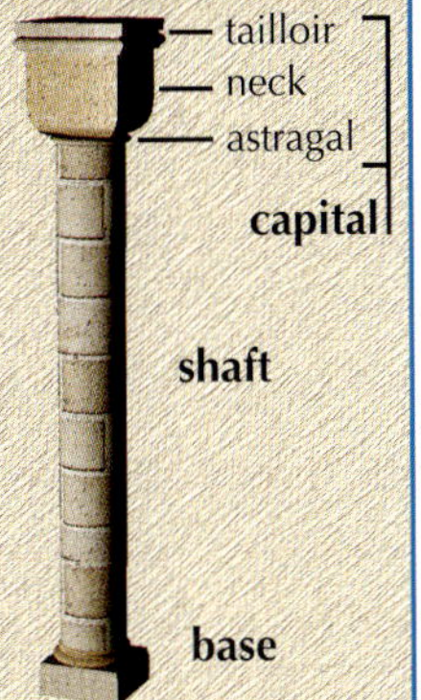

ASTRAGAL. The body of ring-shaped mouldings separating the capital from its support

BASE. Foot of a support. ✔ *The base spreads the vertical load coming from the column and grounds it.*

CAPITAL. From Latin *capitellum*, dimin. of *caput*, "head", "extremity". Decorated and sculpted element placed at the top of a column* or a pilaster*. The capital consists of a **NECK** (the main body of the capital) surmounted by a slab which may be an **abacus** or a tailloir* (medieval capital). ✔ *The capital concentrates the entirety of the forces issuing from the upper parts of the elevation.*

TAILLOIR. Stone table crowning the body of certain capitals. The role of the tailloir, apart from its decorative aspect, was to support the centring* during the building of an arch. ☛ IMPOST*.

Shouldering and buttressing

From the Romanesque* counterforts to the Gothic* flying buttresses, the external structures took on increasing importance.

❶ **Lombard bands** or pilaster strips

Derived their name from the Lombardy masons who influenced the first Romanesque* style. Not thick enough to shoulder*, they could however stiffen the wall.

❷ **Romanesque counterforts**

Not very thick, the Romanesque counterforts shouldered* the edifice at particular points, usually at the level of the springing of the rib vaults.

❸ **Gothic counterforts**

Broader, taller and thicker than the Romanesque counterforts the Gothic counterfort was a shouldering* instrument.

❹ **Flying buttresses**

The flying buttress was the essential buttressing element of Gothic* architecture

(☛ § 1 n° 2, p. 18)

MAIN TERMS

BUTTRESS (to). Is to struggle against a thrust by a counter thrust. Unlike a simple shouldering instrument, a buttress operates an active force.

COUNTERFORT. External masonry reinforcement serving as a shouldering* or a stiffener for a wall or a support.

FLYING BUTTRESS. An element having the shape of a rampant* arch which, springing from a PIER BUTTRESS, buttresses* a vault at a high point. **A TIER OF FLYING BUTTRESSES** is an ensemble of flyers built in a same vertical plan. ✔ *The flying buttress is one of the fundamental elements of Gothic* architecture.*

LOMBARD BANDS (or LESENES). An ensemble of pilasters* joined at their summit by little raised arches (arcade frieze). ☛ illust. above.

PIER BUTTRESS. Solid high body containing the thrust of a flying buttress. ☛ FLYING BUTTRESS.

SHOULDER (to). To oppose to a force* a passive force arising from the sole weight of the masonry (force of inertia). ☛ COUNTERFORT.

WALL BUTTRESS. A very long counterfort* forming a wall perpendicular to the wall it shoulders. Generally pierced by a window, it is like a flyer*, but it is not a buttress*.

OPENINGS

Succeeding to the small openings letting in very little light common in the churches of the Romanesque period, there came the large glazed openings of the Gothic period: the size and shape of openings greatly depended on how the forces were mastered.*

A few Romanesque openings

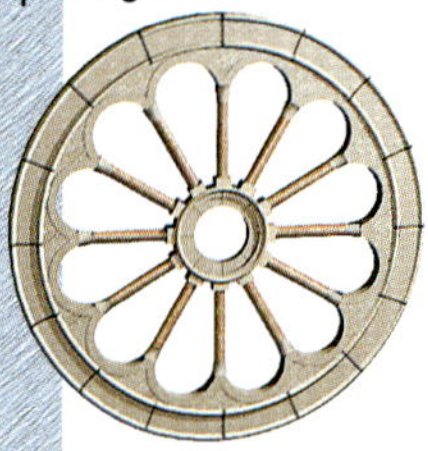

Rose* or wheel* window

Transennae or screen windows

Geminate opening

Opening with en* delit colonnettes

Opening with a double roll* of intrados*

✔ *The only large openings were the* **rose* windows** *and the* **doors** *and these* ***only in the non-bearing walls*** *of the west facade and the arms of the transept* (☛ § 3 p. 9).*

SCREEN WINDOW (or TRANSENNA). Slab of stone pierced in geometrical patterns (lattice-work) set to fill an opening.

❶ Until the Carolingian period, the size of the openings depended little on the structure of the edifice.

Roman concrete vault

The concrete vaults of Roman constructions or the tie* beam timber roofs of Pre-Romanesque churches did not exert any outward thrust* (☛ § 1 page 14). The walls, having no thrust* to contain, could be equipped with large openings (mostly round arched and not splayed), whose position did not obey any strict architectural rule.

❷ The outward thrust of vaults forced the Romanesque* builders to reduce the size of openings considerably.

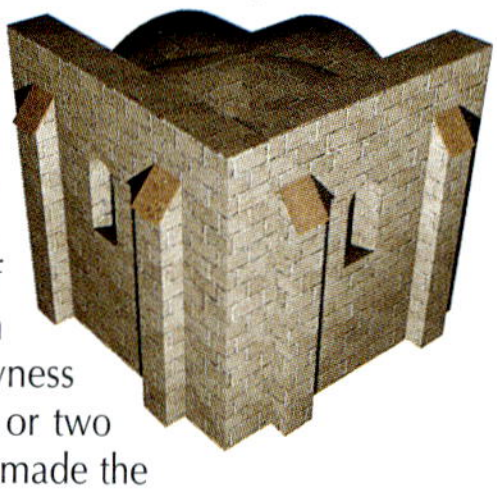

During the Romanesque period, the choice made to vault churches led the builders to make the walls thicker to avoid them collapsing under the pressure of the vaults and to equip the church with a complete structure of resolution of forces (☛ pp. 14 to 17). The risks were such that the clerestory* windows of the central nave were no longer built. As for the walls of the side aisles, where the risks were not as great as in the main aisle, they were never equipped with large openings. The narrowness and the scarcity of openings (in the majority of cases only one or two by bay in the side aisles, and none directly in the central aisle) made the building considerably darker. Several methods therefore were used to palliate this lack of light.

❶ Splaying*.

By cutting the embrasure* of the opening askew, but at the same time keeping the outer opening straight, the Romanesque builders succeeded in letting in more light without weakening the construction. Moreover, splaying can be linked to the development, as yet limited, of stained glass and to the desire to protect the building from unwelcome visitors. Systematically used in numerous churches, it became one of the characteristics of Romanesque* architecture.

With identical outer openings, a non-parallel arrangement of embrasures lets in more light.*

❷ Blind openings.

Fewer openings led to an increase in wall surface. Blind arcades obviously did not remedy the lack of light but provided decoration consisting of false openings which — while sometimes strengthening the stonework — broke the monotony of bare surfaces. Their use became widespread during the Romanesque period.

MAIN TERMS

ARCADE. Free opening consisting of an arch whose jambs* start at the ground level. ☛ GREAT ARCADE.

ARCATURE. Series of little arched* openings.

BLIND (opening, arcature, etc.). Arrangement imitating the presence of an opening.

DOORWAY. Opening allowing coming and going into and out of an edifice, closed by one leaf* or two.

FREE OPENING. Aperture which has neither tracery* or woodwork.

LIGHT. A small opening, generally without filling, for letting in daylight and/or as a decoration. The term is also used to designate any of the perpendicular divisions of a mullioned* window.

OCULUS. From Latin *oculus*, "an eye". A round window used in Romanesque* architecture. Its widespread use for the decoration of facades would give birth to the rose window.

OPENING. Any aperture arranged in a construction and its framing.

ROSE WINDOW. Circular opening with tracery* figuring the shape of a flower. It is a larger oculus reinforced by stone arcatures.

STONEFRAME WINDOW. Opening whose outer ribs form a frame set in a groove of the wall.

WINDOW. An opening equipped with glazing letting light into a building. ☛ CLERESTORY WINDOW.

WHEEL WINDOW. A large rose* window sometimes figuring the spokes of a wheel, filled with stained* glass placed over a doorway*.

*Designation of the openings of a bay**

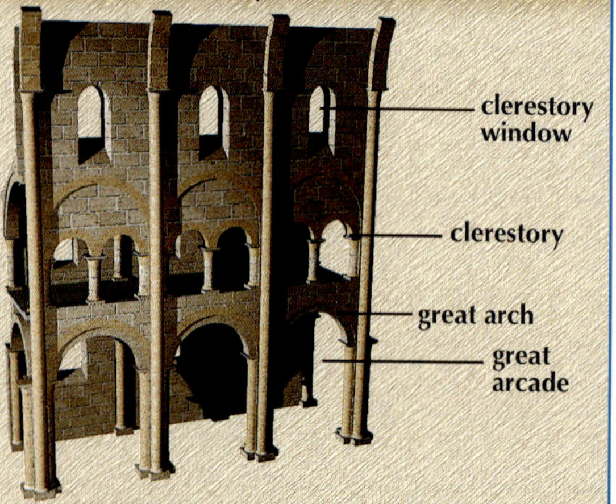

CLERESTORY (or CLEAR STORY). Suite of free openings or of windows lighting a level of elevation along the length of several bays*, separated by supports (columns, piers).

CLERESTORY WINDOW. The highest window of a bay of the central aisle, situated above the side aisles. ✔ *The term is often used to distinguish between Romanesque churches whose central aisle is lit directly and those lit only by the intermediary of the tribunes and the side aisles.*

GREAT ARCADE. An arcade* which, in a bay*, separates the central aisle* from the side aisle*. The arches which cover the great arcades are called **GREAT ARCHES**.

EVOLUTION OF GOTHIC* OPENINGS

First Gothic
1140-1190
The openings as yet have no tracery*

Classical Gothic
1190-1230
The elements of tracery*, at first simple and thick, become independent of the masonry (stoneframe* windows).

Rayonnant Gothic
1230-1360
Tracery* becomes more complex with the appearance of little circular rose windows then of triangular curved patterns.

Flamboyant Gothic
1360 - early XVIth century
Sinuous lines with curves and counter curves seeming to merge with the frame. The mouldings are sharper.

❸ *The Gothic builders broke free from the constraints issuing from the weight of the edifice... But the difficulties they encountered came from the very extent of the surfaces they opened to light.*

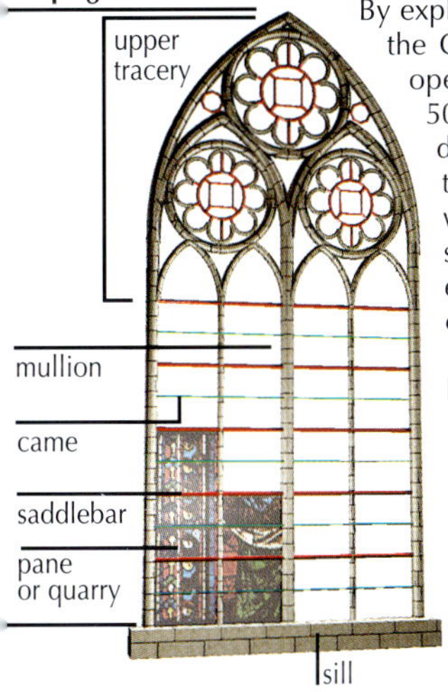

Gothic window. Elements of the structure holding the panes in place and resisting the pressure of the wind.

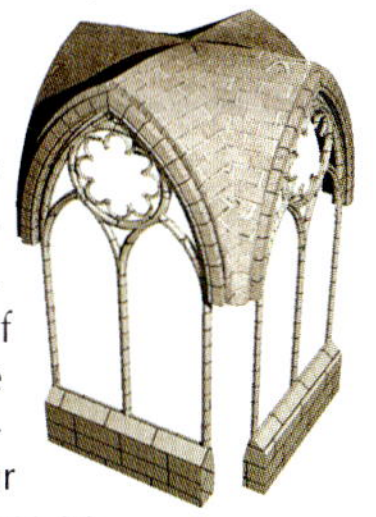

By exploiting to the maximum the possibility of piercing the walls, the Gothic builders made them almost disappear in favour of openings, which soon attained gigantic dimensions (easily 50 m^2) the height under the vaults of churches and of cathedrals in particular seeming to be an object of rivalry. But if the thrust of the vaults was no longer a problem, that of the wind on these immense glazed openings could not be so easily mastered. A gust of wind of approximately 100 km/hour exerts a pressure of about 80 kg per m^2, i.e. more than ten tons on each of the great rose windows of Amiens cathedral (respectively 13 m. and 12.90 m. in diameter). The use becoming now systematic of tracery* is explained by the necessity of keeping the glass panes (the quarries*) in place but also by the necessity of resisting the enormous pressures exerted by the wind. The increase in number of these stone armatures was limited nevertheless by the necessity of letting in light. The builders therefore used more frequently a rigid, thinnish material : **iron**. The metal armature of the panes consisted of **saddlebars** (iron bars fixed in the walls and the mullions*) and other finer strips, the **cames** fixed to the glass panes by little ties of lead so as to stiffen them. In this way the ensemble had a great degree of resistance.

THE ELEMENTS OF AN OPENING

ARCHIVOLT. 1. Body of mouldings carried by the front of an arch over an opening. Around an external opening the archivolt serves as a dripstone*. **2.** Generally designates the whole of the recessed order* of an opening.

EMBRASURE. Empty space between the sides of an opening.

MULLION. Vertical stone member dividing the interior of a Gothic window.

SILL. Horizontal base of a window not reaching the ground. A sill may be flat or **STEPPED.**

SPANDREL. Almost triangular surface between one side of the outer curve of an arch and its enclosing mouldings, wall etc.

SPLAYING. Slantwise piercing of an opening.

STAINED GLASS WINDOW. Ensemble of coloured glass panes fixed by lead strips and fitted inside a window.

TRACERY. Stonework set inside a Gothic window dividing the opening. Tracery consists of mullions* and the network of carved stones (resembling ribs) forming several curving geometrical designs in a Gothic window (usually found in the **UPPER TRACERY**). ☛ illust. above.

TRUMEAU. Piece of wall between two openings pierced on the same level. The term is often wrongly used for the central* pillar which divides the door of a church.

CENTRAL PILLAR. A pillar carrying the springing of the arches (or the lintel*) of a doorway consisting of two geminate* openings.

DOORWAY. When large and decorated may be called a **PORTAL**, consisting of one or several outer doors in the facade* of a church.

JAMB. Vertical side of the opening of a doorway, window or fireplace.

LEAF. Solid panel, sash or grille pivoting on one of its two vertical axes. ✔ *A leaf itself is often mistakenly called a door.*

ORDER (Recessed Order). 1. Small vault* covering the deep embrasure* of an opening. **2.** Each of the concentric arches of an opening.

TYMPANUM. Solid infill of the space above an arch over a doorway. ✔ *The tympanum usually consists of a sculpted surface. This sculpture may be divided into horizontal bands (or* ***registers****) arranged around a theme : the Apocalypse (Moissac) the Last Judgment (Saint Foy of Conques) the Crowning of the Virgin (Notre Dame of Paris), etc.*

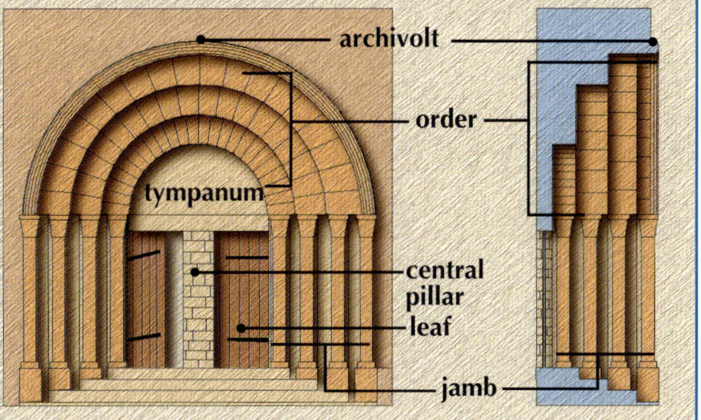

- Elements of a doorway -

TOOLS, MATERIAL...

"Over the course of three centuries, from 1050 to 1350, France had extractec several million tons of stones to build 80 cathedrals, 500 large churches anc some tens of thousands of parish churches. France had carted more stone ir these three centuries than Ancient Egypt during any period of her history."

Jean Gimpel, *Les Bâtisseurs de Cathédrales (The Cathedral builders)*

Stone was the favoured material as much because of its inherent qualities (solidity, hardness, resistance to fire and water) as of the relative easiness of its extraction. Although it was sometimes replaced by timber — in northern Europe — or by brick — when the stone quarries were too far away or exhausted, it had been the fundamental component of the fabric as well as of the vaults since the Xth century (☛ page 26) and was even found on the roofs of churches covered by slate or roofing-stones. If a variety of rocks (basalt, granite or sandstone) were used for building, **limestone** remained the sort most frequently worked : it had the advantage of being widely present geographically and being easily adapted to numerous uses, thanks to its varied textures. In this way blocks of hard limestone were used for building — and the differences of colour sometimes served as decoration — while soft limestone with fine homogeneous texture was used primarily for sculpture. Furthermore, crushed, charred limestone gave quicklime which was transformed into mortar.

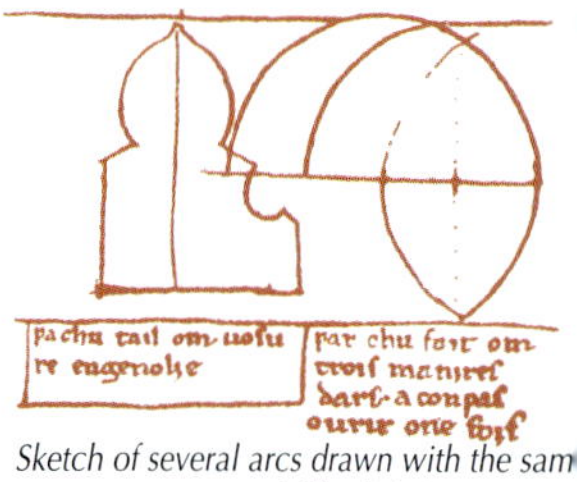

Sketch of several arcs drawn with the sam compass. Villard de Honnecour

The essential purpose of **mortar** was to make the contact faces betweer the stones even. In a drystone wall, i.e. without mortar as the surface of the stones is never completely smootl only a part of each stone bears the weight of what i placed above, a phenomenon which greatly weaken the whole of the edifice. Since it was impossible to cu stones without leaving any asperities, it was morta which **filled in the spaces** between the stones so tha they **jointed** perfectly, thereby **spreading the weigh** over all the surface of the masonry. ☛ § 2 page 14.

Timber was another essential material — for **roof** placed over vaults as well as for **scaffolding** anc **machines** used on the building sites. The major problem facing medieval carpenters was... to find wood The impressive demographic expansion which startec in the XIth century along with the increased use of char coal (used intensively by the emerging foundries) led tc numerous deforestations. A great shortage of large oaks followed : this lack led to the invention of **nev ways of assembling** timber frame roofs needing les large section lumber (☛ page 28).

Iron was the fundamental material for the stone cutters and masons' tools. New techniques improved the soli dity and the "bite" of tools and, thereby, their efficacity Cutting tools soon became the object of fashion creating rivalry between **chisels, axes and hammer** (*sledgehammer*, *axhammer*, *toothed hammer scappling hammer* or *pick*). As for the carpenters, the wielded *axes, saws* and *planes*, pierced large hole with *augers* and smaller ones with *drills*; they some times used *metal nails* but always gave preference tc *wooden pegs* for their assemblages. In parallel to th advances in metal work, a new use was found for iro in the employment of metal tie rods (☛ insert page 18 and in the structures holding the window-panes in plac (☛ § 3 page 31).

MAIN TYPES OF MASONRY

The **shape** and the **quality of the dressing** of the stones along with the way in which they are **laid** vary according to the **regions** and the **period** and the **wealth** of the churches. Certain fundamental types of masonry may be singled out.

Random rubble masonry

Mortar into which stones, brick and pebbles are cast.

Masonry with rubble infilling

Technique which consists in filling with rubble the space between two parallel facings of a wall. In this way fewer dressed stones can be used thus reducing the cost.

Deep course

Two or three parallel facings without rubble infilling.

Single course (a single depth)

Became more and more widespread during the Gothic period, when the walls were no longer bearing.

MAIN TERMS

ASHLAR. Squared hewn stone laid in regular course.

BOND. O.E. *bindan*, "to bind". Conventional pattern in which bricks or stones are laid to ensure strength in structure (☛ insert above).

BRICK. Artificial block of pre-moulded fired clay.

COURSE. Horizontal layer of cut stones. ✔ *Classification according to the height of the courses (height depending on the thickness of the stones) : masonry in* LARGE COURSE *(more than 35 cm),* MEDIUM COURSE *(between 35 and 20 cm),* SMALL COURSE *(less than 20 cm).*

CUTTING. Fitting stones for building. Vaults in cut stone : vaults whose stones hold together by mutual pressure (☛ TO WEDGE), unlike the concrete vaults.

LIME. O.E. *lim*. Calcium hydroxide in powder form. ✔ *The calcining of certain calcareous rocks produces quicklime (extremely corrosive). Slaked lime (lime hydrated then dried) is a component of mortar. Diluted slaked lime becomes whitewash which is used to whiten walls.*

LIMESTONE. Rock composed mainly of calcium carbonate resulting from the sediments of mineral, vegetable and organic matters deposited at the bottom of the sea. ✔ *The rising of sea depths resulted in the emergence of limestone, now solid and compact, in the form of long horizontal layers called* **beds** *(born of successive deposits and so superposed). Most of the beds or layers exploited date from the Mesozoic era. Extracted as quarry stones or ashlar*, limestone must be laid in the same way as it was in the quarry : perpendicular to its natural bed (or laid* EN DELIT*), it cannot support any great weight as it may crumble or split.*

MORTAR. Mixture of slaked lime and an inert substance, usually sand, diluted in water. On drying, mortar becomes solid, the lime becoming limestone. Mortar is also used to roughcast walls as a protection.

ROOFING STONES. Flat stones used like tiles on roofs.

TILE. From Latin *tegula*, from *tegere*, to cover. Thin flat slabs of baked clay (terracotta) used in overlapping rows to roof buildings.

... & BUILDERS

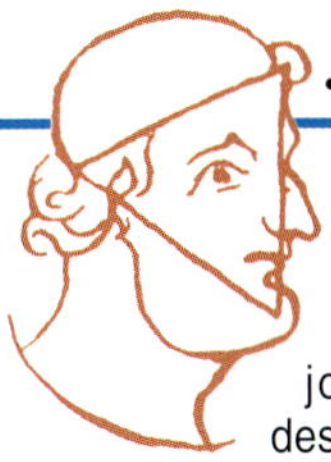

❶ ***Of the men*** of the Middle Ages who invented and built thousands of churches the greater majority remained anonymous — despite "masons' marks" carved in the stone which were not so much signatures as set there for the purpose of payment for tasks owed to the stonehewers. The rare texts of the Romanesque period, written by clerics... mention almost exclusively clerics. Although a document as rare by its precision as the *Pilgrims' Guide* explicitly mentions a cleric as sole architect of Santiago of Compostela and if it is true that the famous Abbot Suger directed operations thus earning the title of *magister operis* (master of works) (☛ insert p. 21), clerics usually participated in construction as **patrons** and administrators of the site. They chose the **master of works** (often the master mason) who planned and directed the construction of the edifice — always subjected to the liturgical imperatives which dictated a specific architecture. This master of works (*architect*, *surveyor* and *engineer* all at the same time) directed and **coordinated** the different craft guilds, with the help of a *parlier* (a speaker, so called because of his knowledge of the different dialects spoken on the site). These builders — ***stone-dressers, master masons, stonecutters, carpenters, sculptors, glaziers, roofers*** and ***labourers*** — were freemen, paid according to the very precise terms of pre-established contracts.

❷ ***The knowledge*** of a master of works was much more a **know-how** than an theoretical knowledge: in order to invent, the master had to take risks, make experiments, always bearing in mind former mistakes and accidents, collapsing of vaults... all the events which were common in the history of building the largest churches. It was also a knowledge founded on **geometry** taken not as an ensemble of theories and equations but as an "**art of line**", a geometry both **strict** (Gothic art built strict figures with very precise angles) and profoundly **empirical**. Certain documents such as the **notebooks** of the famous Villard de Honnecourt consist of mementoes whose figures allow the rediscovery of the "laws" without having recourse to real calculations. Two fundamental instruments were the **compass** and the "**virga**" (from Latin *a stick*, *a rod*): the compass was a tool of major importance allowing the transferring of an identical unity, the drawing of circles thus finding the arcs, the angles, the equilaterals etc. (☛ page 25); the "virga", the stick of the master of works served as a rule for straight lines but also as a **standard measuring rod**, like a yardstick, essential on a building site. Although no unity of measurement was as yet universal — the dimensions were those of certain parts of the body with the *hand* (☛ sketch above), the *foot*, the *cubit* etc. — the absence of common references did not prevent the drawing of **plans**. To understand each other on a building site, the patron and the master of works had at their disposal plans and working models without any precise scale. The plans used for building (when they existed) were of a very relative precision — certain as they were to undergo many modifications on sites that might last over a period of half a century: *line, plumb level, gauge, knotted line*, and *plumb line* were the most reliable instruments on the site. Moreover, the sketches, drawn with compass and square on the walls and ground, known as **working drawings** and drawn on **scale one**, were used for the cutting out of the patterns (the **models**, the **templates**) for the creation of elements of architecture. The search for a greater efficacity and a lower cost soon led the builders to exploit these templates in

order to **standardize** cut stone, voussoirs, elements of tracery etc. in the best possible way. The stone dressers were then capable of cutting the stone directly at the quarry all year round, thereby reducing the load transported (and the cost) along with the economic effect of interruptions on the site due to winter. As for the master of works, he was now free to delegate a number of the tasks to the ***chief masons***: he no longer had to remain on the same site for lengthy periods of time provided he improved the quality of the plans necessary for the coordination of the tasks. The techniques and the know-how which allowed the exact reproduction of a same stone, a same pier, even a same choir were emerging and would end in an appreciable reduction of costs. It therefore became less expensive and so conceivable to build **bigger** and **higher**... up to the limits set by techniques and material. Inevitably there were a few examples of a static reproduction of a same model and there was a potential risk of a veritable standardization, curbed, perhaps, by the will of the builders, whose mentality remained that of craftsmen and artists.

Sketch of the hand as used for measurement from the notebooks of Villard de Honnecourt XIIIth century.

Above yardstick and compass, engraving by Viollet-le-Duc, op. cit.

MACHINES

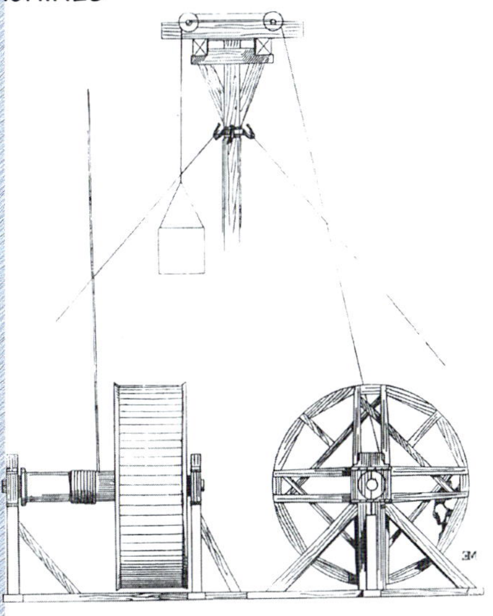

Like churches, which inherited ancient architectural designs, the methods and machines employed by medieval builders were more often than not inspired by the techniques and engines used by the Romans. The machines were essentially **lifting devices**. Placed on the ground or at the top of the building under construction, they were operated by a **manual windlass** or capstan or by great wheels turned on the treadmill system (a ***squirrel cage***) by several men treading inside them. The **quarrier's wheel** operated from the exterior by pulling on uprights set at intervals on its diameter closely resembled this system. By means of **pulleys** installed in series, the force developed was multiplied: a treadmill could hoist more than ten tons. Certain machines, forerunners of present-day cranes, were equipped with an **arm pivoting** on an axis.

DECORATION

Historiated Romanesque capital
Church of the Daurade, Toulouse

As a homage to the gods to whom they were dedicated, temples have always been decorated, and the men of the Middle Ages did not depart from this rule, setting all the resources of their art to the embellishment of their churches.

If the evocative term "**treasure**" indicates the **liturgical furniture**, adorned with precious metals and gems, the veritable testimony to this decoration is more closely linked to the architecture. **Sculpture** is an omnipresent component of this "monumental" decoration: well-preserved, it adorns **capitals***, **tympana***, **portals*** and **modillions***. Medieval churches were more colourful than the uncovered stones, rid of their **roughcast rendering** and **plaster** lead us to believe. In France, these paintings are not well preserved because they are rarely "**frescoes***" but wall-paintings carried out in "**a* tempera**" (distemper). Sculptures and paintings have varied themes: sometimes they are inspired by works of Antiquity or copied from work carried out on other backgrounds such as illuminations or parchments; sometimes they are directly based on readings (especially of the Bible) or from observation; often they spring from the artist's imagination. When their role is educative, the works are illustrations of the lives of the saints, scenes from the Bible or illustrate vices and virtues, symbolizing in this way the precepts of Christian morality. The art of **mosaics** which used the same themes on the walls of Palaeo-Christian and Carolingian churches was less fre quently applied during the Romanesque period an disappeared altogether during the Gothic period. O the other hand during this latter period appeared a ornate pavement in which the **labyrinth** held an im portant place.

N. D. of Paris, elevation of the Virgin portal. Formerly painted and gilded.
E. Viollet-le-Duc, Op. cit.

During the Romanesque* period, sculpture was inse parable from its setting and its tortured forms wer subjected to the architectural surroundings : it rema ned within the field of the **low** — or better the **high relief***. The wall-recesses and the screen* window created a play of light and shadow. The large blin surfaces were reduced by the abundance of **dosse rets***, **transverse* arches** and **Lombard* bands** The latter, which were often elements of "reinforce ment" of minor architectural importance, were usef in giving rhythm to the large blank surfaces of **gutter walls**, belfries, facades and chancels*. Inside th building, the large wall surfaces were adorned wit paintings. The search for aesthetic effect sometime overcame prudence: in the church at **Saint Savin sur-Gartempe**, the transverse* arches of the centr aisle* disappear behind the painter's work whic spreads without interruption over the whole of th vault.

The rib vaulting of Gothic architecture tended to brin about the replacement of walls by **openings**, thu considerably reducing surfaces for painting However, the latter was not confined to what walls re mained or to the vaults : it spread to the interio sculptures and those of the portals. And above al closely affinitive to painting by its play of colours **stained* glass** amplified light and became an art i its own right: a technical challenge (☛ p. 31) a much as an artistic one, these assemblages of colou red glass filled the openings left free by the new equ librium of the buildings. As for sculpture, it becam **detached* from its supports**, at least in some part of the church. Isolated in wall-recesses, under ston canopies*, statues — which showed an increasin realism — covered portals* and flying* buttress piers or stood upright under the **arcades*** of the narro facade galleries, **the kings' galleries** (☛ page 21 the church itself was treated like a great sculpture Beyond the purely technical aspect, the forests o **flying* buttresses** of some Gothic cathedrals* sho an undeniable aesthetic research : the increase o elements which were superfluous with regard to a chitectural stability — like the ribs of many vaults — are testimonies to such a research (☛ page 18).

MAIN TERMS

A TEMPERA (distemper). Unlike that of frescoes, the pigments are fixed by glue or size onto a dry coating. ✔ *After a while, these glues deteriorate the paintings gradually fade.*

CANOPY. Projecting covering to protect a statue.

DETACHED STATUE. A free standing statue, detached from its background and in this differs from low-reliefs, half-reliefs and high-reliefs.

FRESCO. From Italian *cool, fresh.* Painting done rapidly on wet plaster so that the pigments penetrate it and become fixed as it dries. ☛ A* TEMPERA. ✔ *When the chemical reaction which re-transforms calcium oxide (lime) into calcium carbonate (limestone) operates, these pigments are trapped in the plaster itself and can no longer be separated from it.*

MODILLION. Corbel, projecting stone, usually sculpted, supporting the elements of a cornice. The spaces between modillions are called **METOPES** (sometimes sculpted).

MOSAIC. Arrangement of small multicoloured pieces (or *tessera:* cubes, strips, irregular-shaped fragments) of stone, marble, terra-cotta, enamel, glass or metal, held together by mortar or resin forming a design. ✔ *There are pavement mosaics or wall mosaics.*

PLASTER. Thin layer usually of fatlime (of low clay content) used as a finishing on roughcast rendering.

RELIEF (LOW-) (or basso-relievo). Sculpture projecting slightly from the background to which it is attached. If the projection is equal to half the depth of the subject, the work is in **HALF-RELIEF** (mezzo-relievo). When the projection is equal to the depth of the subject, the work is in **HIGH-RELIEF** (or alto-relievo).

ROUGHCAST (rendering). Coat of mortar applied to a building.

SOME POINTS OF REFERENCE

CANON. From eccles. Latin *canonicus*, "conforming to a religious Order". Designates a cleric, member of a chapter of certain churches (cathedral, basilica) in which he celebrates the daily religious service. ✔ *Unlike monks canons might also have pastoral activities outside their community.*

CHAPTER. From Latin *capitulum* diminutive of *caput*, "head". 1. Heading of a text, or main division of a book. **2.** By extension, an assembly of canons or monks during which a chapter of the Rule is read. ✔ *The chapter is the veritable governing body which makes autonomous decisions by deliberation and in certain cases may oppose the will of the bishop.* **3.** Place where the chapter assembles (meaning n° 2) hence the term : *chapter house.*

CLERIC. 1. Whoever enters into holy orders by receiving the tonsure. **2.** Whoever belongs to the hierarchy of the Church. The body of clerics is called the clergy. Of the same origin, a clerk is a literate person or lay officer of a cathedral, a college chapel etc., cf. chapter clerk.

CONSTANTINE I the Great (c. 285 - 337). Reigned over the western part of the Roman Empire and later over the whole of the Empire after overthrowing the eastern Augustus. His mother (the future Saint Helena) being a Christian, he protected Christianity and he made it a state religion — this new religion being more likely to establish his authority by allowing him to become an emperor by divine right.

LAY. In a general sense, that which is not ecclesiastical. **1.** A **LAY BROTHER** (or SISTER) is one who, living in a monastery or convent, was not pronounced holy vows and is entrusted with manual tasks (especially agriculture ones). **2.** Some one devoted to religion pronouncing vows without acceding to a religious function bound by a sacrament (e.g priesthood).

MONK. Origin Old English, *munuc*, from Greek *monos*, "alone". Originally laymen who, solitary (anchorite) or more frequently in a community (coenobite) lead a religious life outside secular society. From the XIth century onwards, more and more monks became priests by receiving the sacrament. Prayer — *opus dei*, "the work of God" — was their main activity.

NOVICE. He or she who is being prepared to become a monk (or nun) but who has not yet pronounced the vows of obedience, poverty and chastity imposed by the monastic Rule.

ORDER. 1. Group of persons living in religious association after having made solemn vows (the forms of religious life consisting only of simple vows are called Congregations). **2.** Group of monks obedient to the same Rule living in a monastery placed under the direction of a mother abbey. The **CLUNIAC ORDER**, dependent on the Benedictine abbey of Cluny founded in 910, was the model for almost all abbeys until the XIIth century, until it lost its influence because of its too great wealth which was too obvious even in the gigantic splendour of the architecture of its church (☛ page 3). The **CISTERCIAN ORDER** dependent on the abbey of Citeaux founded in 1098 : in the first half of the XIIth century, Saint Bernard of Clairvaux spread the Cistercian Rule (which preached the respect of the Cistercian Order by a return to the observance of poverty, silence and manual labour) and recommended a severe unadorned monastic environment. There also developed **MILITARY RELIGIOUS ORDERS** tied to the "Peace of God" and the Crusades : the Knights Templars and Hospitallers, and the **MENDICANT ORDERS** : friars who relied solely on alms and were implanted in the towns (Predicant Friars such as the Dominicans and the Franciscans) : it was under the influence of the Dominicans, for example, that an increasing number of **HALL CHURCHES** were built, following the southern tradition of the church with a single nave and with aisles of the same height in elevation, allowing the Dominicans to preach in closer contact with the people and thus to fight against heresy more efficiently.

PARISH. From Greek *paroika*, a stay in a foreign country, a metaphor applied to Christians who considered themselves citizens of the next world, and only passing through this world here on earth. **1.** Ecclesiastic territorial circonscription under the authority of a priest. **2.** By metonymy, the term is used for the whole of the faithful living in this territory. ✔ *The church in which the priest exercises his ministry is called the* **PARISH CHURCH.**

PRIORY. Small monastery dependent on a mother abbey and governed by a **PRIOR** appointed by the abbot. The term **PRIOR** also designates a monk who governs an abbey during the absence of the abbot.

RULE. From Latin *regula*, "a straight stick" via Old French *reule*. Written code fixing the way of life of the religious subjected to it. From the IXth century onwards, the principal Rules applied in France were those of Saint Benedict (founder of Montecassino in 529) for monks called from then on **Benedictines** and those of Saint Augustine for canons. ✔ **REGULAR** *(whoever follows a Rule) is opposed to* **SECULAR** *(whoever lives in the world and is not subjected to a strict monastic enclosure).*

TRENT (Council of)**.** Assembly of bishops summoned by the Pope in Trento (northern Italy) between 1545 and 1563 under the influence of Charles V to oppose the progress of the Protestant Reformation. This council clarified and re-defined the fundamental questions of dogma, ethics and discipline of Catholic doctrine and reaffirmed the sacred character of the priesthood and the sacraments. In addition, it abolished the use of partitions in churches

ORIENTATION

ANTERIOR, POSTERIOR, LATERAL. Adjectives used to situate the elevations of a building in relation one to another. In a basilican church that which is **opposite the chancel** is **ANTERIOR** and that which is **towards the chancel** is **POSTERIOR**. The **LATERAL** elevations join the anterior and posterior elevations.

ELEVATION. Vertical face or the ensemble of vertical faces of a building or main part of a building.

FACADE. Exterior elevation.

LONGITUDINAL. That which is lengthwise i.e. the longest dimension of an object or a building.

OCCIDENT. The West. When a church has two architectural choirs, one may be turned in the direction of the West (Occident) and the other in direction of the East (Orient) ; this is the case of certain early medieval churches, a church is said to be "*occidented*" only when the liturgical choir faces the West.

ORIENT (to). Literally, "to turn towards the East" (the Orient). Most of the churches of western Europe were oriented i.e. the choir of these churches was built towards the East, from where Christ will come at the end of time…

TRANSVERSE. Which crosses, perpendicular to the largest dimension.

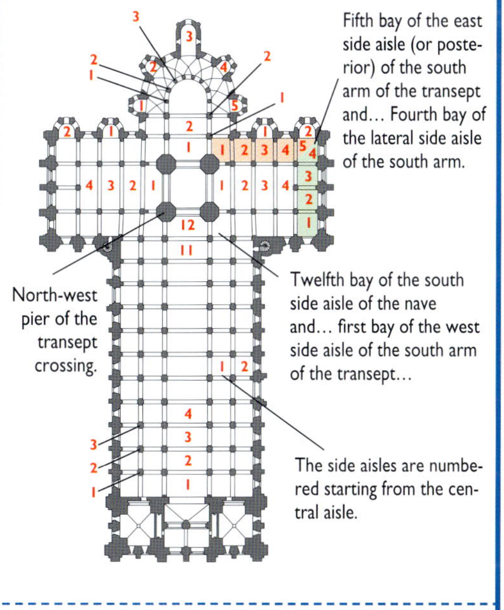

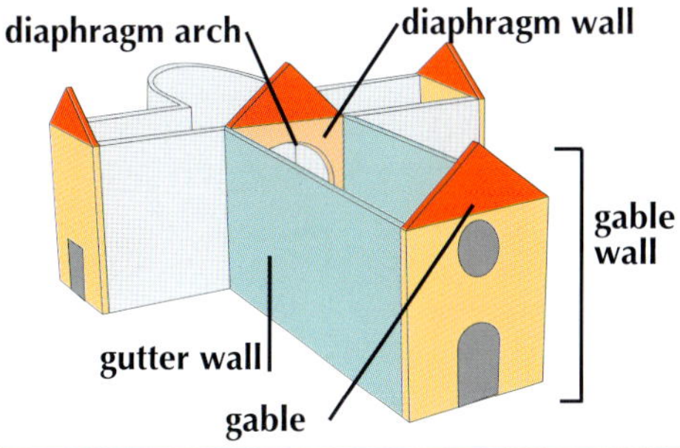

GUTTER WALL. From Latin *gutta*, "a drop", via Old French *goutière*. Wall which carries the gutter of a slope of a roof, perpendicular to the gable wall.

GABLE. Upper part of a wall, parallel to the trusses of the timberwork and closing the front of a roof. In church architecture, the gable, usually triangular in shape, has a negligeable bearing role. The **GABLE WALL** is an exterior wall carrying a gable. It is generally a facade wall. The **DIAPHRAGM WALL** (form Greek *diaphragma*, "separation") is an interior gable wall mounted on a transverse arch, the **DIAPHRAGM ARCH** and may serve as a firebreak.

INDEX

The numbers in bold type ref
to the definition of the terr